THE SCRAPLOOK

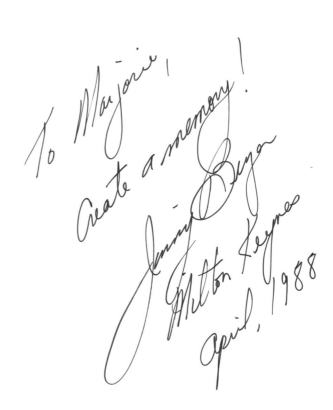

To Marjorie,
Create a memory!
Jenny Bryan
Milton Keynes
April, 1988

THE SCRAP LOOK

Designs, Fabrics, Colors and
Piecing Techniques for Creating Multi-Fabric Quilts

JINNY BEYER

EPM
PUBLICATIONS, INC.

**Library of Congress
Cataloging-in-Publication Data**

Beyer, Jinny.
    The scrap look.

    Bibliography: p.
    1. Quilting. I. Title.
TT835.B45   1985   746.9'7   85-16153
ISBN 0-914440-86-1

Book and cover design by Tom Huestis

CONTENTS

Other books by Jinny Beyer

PATCHWORK PATTERNS

THE QUILTER'S ALBUM OF BLOCKS & BORDERS

MEDALLION QUILTS

A SIX-MINUTE MILE

The Charm of the Past, the Rage of Today

Spread out one of Grandmother's old scrap quilts at a family gathering and sit back and listen. "Oh, look at that piece. It was my first prom dress. I made an apron out of that one—look at Julie's blouse."

The nostalgia attached to quilts for anyone who grew up with them is overwhelming. And as beautiful as a white on white can be, or a Baltimore Album appliqué, or various other "best" quilts made for display or special occasions, it is the so-called scrapbag quilts that evoke the most memories and have the most charm.

On hearing the words "scrapbag quilts," we conjure up images of women painstakingly cutting the good parts from worn out clothes or sorting through pieces of fabric left over from sewing, salvaging bits and pieces for quilts. Certainly many quilts have been made in this manner—particularly during the formative years of our country. There are not many of them left. They were simply used up.

The stories of scrap quilts live on, however: of how frontier women would piece scraps into door quilts to cut down on drafts or into heavy covers to keep their families warm. Some city women who felt quilting unworthy of them nevertheless would not waste their scraps; they gave them to the church to be made into quilts for the poor, or they sent them out to others to be made into quilts.

Lenice Bacon wrote the following about her childhood in the early 1900s: *"Quilts were a part of my life even during the years when they were not in fashion. In that section of Tennessee where I grew up in the early part of the twentieth century, quilts served as a suitable lightweight bedcovering in a moderate climate. We had a goodly supply for 'everyday wear,' but they were not made at home. They were made by the Witt sisters, two nice maiden ladies who lived in the country and during the winter months 'pieced quilt tops on the half.' That is, for half the scraps my mother provided they would piece quilt tops for her and the other scraps were theirs to use for themselves. In the fall of the year,*

Mother took materials left from the family sewing to them; these included bits from our outgrown cotton dresses. Then, in the spring, the finished quilt tops were picked up."[1]

She goes on to say that batting and fabric for the backing were purchased and everything was taken to an elderly lady who did the quilting.

The scrapbag was a part of every household, and contained good parts of used clothing and pieces left over from making new family garments. It was certainly the place where a child found the first pieces to try a hand at needlework, or where a woman found the necessary material to do her mending.

In colonial times before printed fabrics were readily available women had to make many of their quilts strictly from scraps. They made the most of the scraps by lavishing attention on overall designs and color. Carrie Hall and Rose Kretsinger tell about this in their book, *The Romance of the Patchwork Quilt in America*:

"In the Colonial bedroom, where the bed was the principal piece of furniture, the quilt, often startling, yet seldom other than beautiful, was the central motif, the object of first consideration, both in pattern and coloring, and other decorations were of minor importance; hence there was no thought of matching the quilt to any particular decorative scheme. It was made of whatever the scrapbag contained, or if an especial pattern was to be copied, the materials were hand-dyed for that particular design."[2]

After cotton goods became available in this country, respect for the leftover pieces continued:

"Quiltmakers could not easily forget the strict embargoes and heavy taxes placed on them for the use of certain fabrics, especially the cotton prints from Calcutta. Nor could they forget the tedious and backbreaking hours spent at the loom in former days. So, the scrapbag remained one of the most prized items in every household, and neighbors delighted in swapping interesting bits of rare materials."[3]

In the days when the next ship from Europe was long in coming quilts were made almost exclusively from scraps and salvageable parts of used clothing. However, once goods became available, women would have wanted to improve the quality and longevity of their quilts. Making them with the remains of used clothing could hardly have produced a product that lasted long. If some parts of the clothing had already worn out, the good parts would probably not last a lot longer either. Marie Webster writes of the quality of material in her book, *Quilts, Their Story and How to Make Them*:

"The type of quilt that may be called distinctively American was substantial in character; the material that entered into its construction was serviceable, of a good quality of cotton cloth, or handwoven linen, and the careful work put into it was intended to stand the test of time. . . . Some cottons were dyed by the quilt makers themselves, if desirable fast shades could not be readily procured otherwise. The fundamental idea was to make a quilt that would withstand the greatest possible amount of wear . . . the painstaking

needlework required to produce a quilt deserved the best of material for its foundation."[4]

Perhaps a myth has grown up about scrapbag quilts. The first settlers or the very poor or frugal housewives may have relied strictly on scraps for their quilts; but I believe that equally as many, or more, scrap quilts made in the 19th and 20th centuries were made from fabrics carefully saved, traded and, yes, even <u>purchased</u> with specific quilts in mind.

By the 1850s with roller printing well established in this country, huge varieties of cotton goods were available at a reasonable price. The Orlofskys believe that by this time the practice of purchasing fabric for quilts was widespread. "Materials were bought specifically for the purpose of making a quilt," they write. "The housewife was no longer dependent upon the accumulation of scraps of different colors and sizes in her scrap bag to create a specific pattern or design."[5]

Laurel Horton further substantiates their view when she states, "Lola's quilt represents the successful incorporation of scraps into a planned color scheme. This is characteristic of many late nineteenth century quilts in South Carolina. . . . Quilts represented an investment of time and effort which was normally matched with an investment in materials. After about 1870, a virtual explosion of scrap quilts, especially in the upstate area around Greenville, irrevocably altered the definition of the quilt. Then, in addition to fancy quilts made to exhibit fine needlework, there were quilts which became an eco-nomical response to an abundance of inexpensive fabrics. The existence of scrap quilts paralleled the development of textile mills in the Upstate. These factories provided not only a variety of locally produced fabrics but also the cash income with which to buy them."[6]

Even the very poor would scrape together the necessary money to buy fabric. In 1915, in writing of the importance of quilting to Appalachian Mountain women, Marie Webster reported: "The mountain women seldom dye their own fabrics any more. They bring in a few chickens or eggs to the nearest village, and in exchange obtain a few yards of precious coloured calico for their quilts."[7]

Lenice Bacon tells of a young wife and mother, Elizabeth B. Welch, who in 1848 stayed at home working in a textile mill in Massachusetts while her husband went to California to find gold. "While he was gone, she used her meager savings to purchase print cloth and pieced together a Rising Sun quilt as a welcome-home gift."[8]

Ruth Finley also told of women purchasing fabrics for quilts in describing a beautiful early 19th-century quilt. "Scraps may have gone into its making, but there was enough of the same material to carry out a premeditated color scheme. In other words, the cloth was cut to suit the quilt, not the quilt to suit the cloth. . . . In time, as economic stress lessened, this practise (of purchasing fabric for a quilt) also became prevalent in New England, but it developed much earlier in the Southern colonies."[9]

Jeannette Lasansky has described a

quilt made by either Dora Mensch Musser or Sarah Stahl Snyder around 1900 and told of the quiltmaking done in that family:

"The organization of all this family's quilts is superb. . . . It is apparent in viewing the total output of these women that they frequently purchased fabric specifically for their quilts. This is true of nearly all the area's appliqués and of a good proportion of the pieced quilts no matter how simple."[10]

As the scrap look became popular, fabric pieces were both traded and purchased to get more variety in the quilts. By the 1930s the sale of multiple fabrics for scrap quilts had become commonplace. The 1934 Sears Roebuck catalog offered cellophane-wrapped packages of a variety of fast-colored quilt patches. Each 12-ounce package was said to contain enough material for an average size quilt top. With two patchwork designs and quilting chart thrown in, the package cost 23¢!

All we need to do is to look at the backing on an old quilt to confirm that it was purchased for the quilt. I have seen a few patched backings, but many are beautiful prints of all one fabric. The fabric certainly would have been enough for a dress or blouse, and most likely was purchased specifically for the quilt to coordinate with the scraps. Many so-called scrap quilts also use a common fabric as a setting block or as a wide border such as the one shown in Color plate 1.

Look at the quilt in Photograph 1. At first glance, one would say it is the epitome of a scrap quilt. It has many different fabrics, some of them even pieced

together to get a swatch large enough for the pattern piece. A closer look reveals that actually no two patches are the same. There are 528 different fabrics in that quilt! It seems very improbable that the person who made it would not have had enough of many of the fabrics to use these several times. What she was doing was making a Charm quilt, a type of quilt that has been neglected for many years but about which more and more information is surfacing. I have devoted all of Chapter V to it.

Whether women got the fabric for their scrap quilts out of scrapbags or bought it new or traded with friends, they did not put these quilts together in a haphazard way. The graphic quality, the continuity of design and color in yesterday's scrap quilts is spectacular. Women then enjoyed working with many fabrics to create an overall scrap look just as we do today. And they had an advantage over us a hundred or more years ago in that most scraps left over from clothes sewing were compatible and could be integrated successfully into a quilt. Dyes were softer then and, as a result, fabrics blended together better. Also, the fabrics were made of natural fibers, usually all cotton, still the preference of most quiltmakers.

Today making quilts out of scraps left over from sewing is almost impossible. In the first place, women are not making nearly as many clothes as they once did. Evidence of this is in the large number of fabric stores and fabric mills that have gone out of business in recent years. Some pattern companies, in an effort to make up for their losses, are

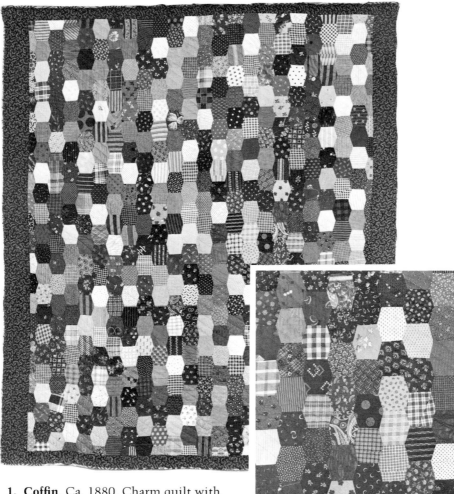

1. Coffin. Ca. 1880. Charm quilt with 528 different pieces. The detail shows the variety in the fabrics. Author's collection.

printing several sizes in one pattern now. More and more women are in the work force and finding less time to make their own clothes. What free time they have, they would rather spend on making something more creative. Women who do sew their own clothes wind up with a variety of left overs— polyesters, rayons, seersuckers, corduroys, satins, silks and all manner of blends that don't work effectively in traditional quilts. Though my own solution to that problem may not be acceptable to others, I offer it for whatever use it may have for some. When my daughter was small and I was still making her clothes, I would take her straight to the 100 percent cotton section and pick out several fabrics that I felt would also look good in a quilt. I then let her choose from among those a fabric for her dress.

The last 15 years have seen a renewed interest in quilting, perhaps unmatched in any time before. Now quilts are primarily made of purchased fabric, bought specifically for quiltmaking. The so-called scraps we use are leftovers from making other quilts or new fabrics purchased for quiltmaking that we haven't even cut into yet.

FABRIC ADDICTS

As scrap quilts have gained in popularity, I have wondered why the sudden interest and decided that one reason has to do with quilters' fabric inventory. In the very early days of our country women salvaged anything they could to make quilts. Now we are trying to use up the fabric we already have on hand to make room for more. People who get involved in quiltmaking develop an obsession for fabric. When we enter a fabric store we can't help going crazy at the sight of the newest line; rarely will we walk out of the door empty-handed. My husband once observed me unpacking some newly purchased fabric. I ran my hands over it, stared at it, held it at a distance, even smelled the newness of it. He said I reminded him of an alcoholic caressing a bottle.

Quilters go through stages in developing their fabric collections. The first year or two we buy fabric only for specific projects and usually quarter yard pieces at a time. When I was in that stage I stored my fabrics in some of those plastic sweater boxes that come from variety stores. I had a box for blues and greens, one for reds and pinks, another for browns and blacks

and one for yellows and rusts. The last one was for miscellaneous colors. I soon graduated to one box for each color. But then it happened several times when I was working on a project that I would use up the entire quarter yard and couldn't find any more to match it. I started "saving" fabrics, being afraid to use them for fear I wouldn't have any left when I really needed them. The solution, of course, was to buy more than a quarter yard when I purchased fabrics. I graduated from quarter yard cuts to half yard, then to yard cuts and finally three yards. Sometimes, depending on the fabric, I would buy eight to ten yards at a time, and occasionally a whole bolt. My storage system grew from plastic boxes to green garbage bags, to large cardboard storage boxes. With the exception of whole bolts of fabric, I now have my fabrics stored in these boxes with two boxes for each color.

A few years ago when my husband and I were getting interested in antiques, I thought of a wonderful kind of collection to start: trunks. If I collected trunks with flat tops, preferably those that can have lamps and other items sitting on top, people wouldn't bother to look inside. I don't believe my husband would mind if he knew how much fabric I really have, but even so it gets embarrassing after a while and space does get limited.

My situation is not unique. Everywhere I travel people tell me about their passion for fabric. One woman said her husband threatened to divorce her if she brought any more into the house. So she said, "I just don't bring it in the house anymore. I store it in the trunk of my car. He never looks in there." Another woman told me that when she moved she labeled most of her fabric boxes "kitchen" because she knew her husband would never help her unpack the kitchen and she didn't want him to know how much fabric she had.

Two women were overheard talking at the merchant mall of a quilt conference. One of them said to the other, "Oh, I can't stand it, look at those beautiful fabrics. Oh dear, what will I do? I have to have some, but I told myself I wouldn't buy any more until I used up some of what I have."

Her friend calmly looked at her and said, "I must be missing something. Are we supposed to use it?"

One woman solved her fabric storage problem in a unique way. I watched her stand in line at a fabric store with her arms full of bolts of fabrics. The woman in front of her was getting quarter yard cuts of everything. As each quarter yard was cut she said, "Save that bolt, I'm going to have some too." When it was her turn she said, "None of that quarter yard business for me. If I like it enough to buy it, I need enough to do something with. Give me three yards of everything. I never buy less than three yards."

Her bill totaled almost $300. Aghast, I asked where she stored all her fabric.

"My husband wouldn't mind if he knew how much I have," she said, "Anyway, I earn my own money and he doesn't need to know everything. My neighbor came over one day and we took her van to the lumber yard and

bought long boards. Then she helped me get a ladder to the little hole in the ceiling that goes to the rafters. We laid the boards over the insulation and I store it all up there. My husband has no idea that I have all that fabric up there."

One woman felt no need to apologize for her many fabrics or make excuses for it. She said, "The only justification I need for buying a new fabric is that I don't already have it."

These are not isolated examples. Many of us have accumulated huge inventories of fabric and are running out of places to store it, or we are feeling guilty every time we walk into the house with more fabric. Worse yet, our tastes have changed over the years. We look at some of those pieces bought so enthusiastically when we took the plunge into buying three yard pieces, and now we wonder why we bought such garishness. We discover more and more fabrics that we once purchased, that we no longer like, that don't fit into a quilt and that we wish we had never bought. They have sat there for five years with barely a piece cut out.

Is it any wonder that scrapbag quilts have become so popular? We think of them as a great way to use so many different fabrics. Of course, a quilt that uses 50 or more different fabrics is not going to take a very big chunk out of any one three yard piece. And if you haven't liked the fabric in any project you have tried it in so far, it's not apt to work miraculously into your scrapbag quilt.

So what can be done with all those fabrics you don't like? Many people have discovered that some that are too strong in color or contrast can be transformed by dyeing them either in a strong tea solution or a commercial fabric dye.

To tea dye fabric, use three or four tea bags to each two quarts of boiling water and simmer the cloth in it for a few minutes. Then let it soak in the solution until the desired color is obtained. Make sure there is enough liquid in the pan so the fabric is completely saturated and will turn an even color. Wash and iron the fabric and it is ready to use.

You might not feel so guilty about bringing home more fabric if you get rid of those you don't like. You might as well realize that there are some that you may never use. Get them out and give them to the Goodwill, the local church or the school art department. Most quilt groups have fabric swap baskets, where you can leave a piece of fabric and trade it for something else. If you have a three yard piece that has been around for five years and has never worked, why not take it to the fabric swap? Some other quilter may come along and be as delighted with the fabric as you were when you first bought it. It may work in her scheme of things or she may have it hanging around for the next five years until she decides she can't use it either.

Some fabrics can surprise you—instead of looking at the fabric as a whole, look at just parts of it. One segment cut into tiny squares or triangles may be great, even though the whole piece may be busy.

Once you have sorted through your fabrics, be prepared to face the fact that no matter how many you still have on hand you are probably going to have to—or want to—purchase more for your scrap look quilt.

MAKING MEMORIES

Our desire to use up some of our accumulated fabrics may be at the base of the current interest in scrap quilts. But I believe there is yet another explanation. Although any design can be made into a pleasing scrap quilt, most people think of scrap quilts as being made of repeat units or one-patch designs. They may regard them therefore as "simpler" quilts—ones to relax with. Although there are certainly many "masterpiece" scrap quilts, particularly in terms of graphics and color, the idea of simplicity is there and may be part of the appeal. With the wealth of information in magazines and books about quilting, with the elevation of the quilt from the bed to the gallery wall, many quiltmakers are feeling driven to create and innovate. Under such pressure there comes a desire to back off, to want to sit down and relax. As my friend Nancy Johnson says, "There are times when you just want to sew." I agree. Nothing relaxes me more than to be able to pick up a basket of pieces and sew—not plan, design, cut or create . . . just sew.

To most quilters the scrap quilt symbolizes better than any other type all the warmth and joy of American quilting. It is humble, unpretentious, down-home—the kind of quilt that memories are wrapped into.

FOOTNOTES

1. Bacon, Lenice Ingram, *American Patchwork Quilts*, p. 16–19.
2. Hall, Carrie A. and Kretsinger, Rose G.,
   *The Romance of the Patchwork Quilt in
   America*, p. 28.
3. Bacon, p. 111.
4. Webster, Marie D., *Quilts, Their Story
   and How to Make Them*, p. 83–84.
5. Orlofsky, Patsy and Myron, *Quilts in
   America*, p. 58.
6. Horton, Laurel and Myers, Lynn Robertson, *Social Fabric; South Carolina's Traditional Quilts*, p. 20–21.
7. Webster, p. 75–76.
8. Bacon, p. 94–98.
9. Finley, Ruth E., *Old Patchwork Quilts
   and the Women Who Made Them*,
   p. 39–40.
10. Lasansky, Jeannette, *In the Heart of
    Pennsylvania, 19th and 20th Century
    Quiltmaking Traditions*, p. 66.

Fabric and Color Use In Creating the Scrap Look

A beautiful old scrap quilt attains its distinction through a rich blending of contrasts, textures and colors. Quiltmakers today are trying to achieve that "look" with modern day fabrics. In order to do so successfully we need to look at the old quilts and see what types of fabrics were used or were not used. The old fabrics did not have as many bold colors as many of ours. There were not many small multi-colored prints—those we think of as "calico". Actually the calico prints of the past were mostly of two colors. The old quilts used large prints as well as small ones. Most of the fabrics did not have strong contrasts between lights and darks.

No matter what the type of pattern, there is a challenge in trying to get a variety of fabrics to work together compatibly. I have always enjoyed making quilts using many different fabrics, and would find it monotonous to select a few coordinated prints and make all the blocks exactly the same. It is more exciting to do each block a little differently. Some blocks turn out better than others, but the whole process can teach one better ways to work with fabrics. Finding the right balance between contrasts, textures and colors is the key to creating a pleasing quilt, and it is important to consider each component individually, even to try some exercises with fabrics.

CONTRAST

Creating the proper balance between lights and darks, actually discovering which fabrics are dark and which are light, is not easy. Very often a person will have assembled a wonderful group of fabrics for a quilt but when the first block is put together it falls short; the design doesn't stand out at all. The problem is usually caused by improper placement of light, medium and dark fabrics. One should first look at a design and decide which part should stand out. That part should either be the darkest fabric with the lightest next to it, or vice versa.

When I begin a project I work strictly with black and white sketches, deciding which parts of the design are to be dark, medium or light colored fabrics. I work only with a black pen, coloring the darks black, leaving the lights white, making dots for the mediums and putting stripes in areas where I may use a border print. To me, getting the contrast right is more important than color or texture, because if the design does not stand out, the whole impact of the quilt is lost.

When starting a block style quilt such as "Castle Keep," (Color plate 8) I will make several drawings of the design, coloring each one in different versions of black, white and medium. (In the case of this quilt it was the star I wanted most to stand out, so in coloring the design I made sure that the points of the star were in sharp contrast to the shapes next to them.) I then photocopy the drawings several times and paste the various versions together to find the one I like the best. Sometimes, as in the case of "Castle Keep," I will use two different colored versions, alternating them every other one. Diagrams 1, 2 and 3 show how the individual blocks are colored and how several of them look when alternated. If you squint and hold the diagram at arm's length, you can see the secondary pattern that the lights form when several blocks are put together. If the light/dark pattern is followed when putting the fabrics together, the same pattern will show up in the quilt.

With overall quilt patterns, such as one-patch designs, it is usually easier to decide upon light and dark placement. Take, for instance, the pattern "Thousand Pyramids." (See Color plates 18 and 19.) This popular design is usually pieced with all the dark triangles pointing in one direction and all the lights pointing in the other (Diagram 4).

The "Tumbling Blocks" pattern uses darks, mediums and lights with the darks always on one side, the mediums on another and the lights on the third (as in Diagram 5).

Diagram 1

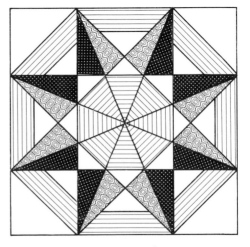

Diagram 2

Diagram 3

Diagram 4

Diagram 5

DETERMINING DARK, MEDIUM, LIGHT

Whatever the design, I always make several black and white sketches. It is only after I am satisfied with the dark, medium, light contrast in a sketch that I will go on to fabrics, gathering the ones I want to use and sorting them into dark, medium and light piles. As I said above, this sorting isn't as easy as it may seem. In the first place, the darks, mediums and lights are all relative to the general group of fabrics you are working with. Someone working with pastels will have a much lighter fabric for a dark than someone working with much darker fabrics. In Diagram 6, for example, the darkest fabric in the

group on the left is also the lightest fabric in the group on the right.

The print of the fabric can affect the general tone. A fabric with a very dark, solid background but with a light design may end up in the medium toned pile.

Color can play tricks on you. Let's say you have two different fabrics, one navy and one red. Your general instincts may tell you that the navy is dark and the red is medium, but in actual fact it may be that the value is the same on both. Don't make the mistake of putting all of your red fabrics in the medium pile and all of the blues in the dark pile. Some of each, depending upon the intensity of the color, the value and the print, will end up in the

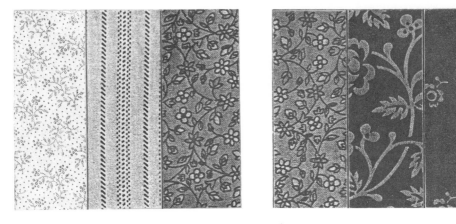

Diagram 6

dark, medium and light piles.

One of the easiest ways to sort the fabrics into dark, medium and lights is to drape them next to each other over a sofa or a chair and then stand a good distance away and squint at them. If you wear glasses, take your glasses off so the fabrics become a little fuzzy. From a distance they look much different, and it becomes easier to sort them. If you are still having difficulty with the choices, and you have access to a Polaroid camera, take a black and white photograph. The value differences show up well when you eliminate color; also if the contrast shows up well in black and white, it will work well in color too. Another trick some people use to help in sorting fabrics is to look at them through a piece of red glass or transparent plastic (such as a lens or filter for a camera); it mutes the color and lets the contrasts show.

Once you have your fabrics divided into darks, mediums and lights, remember they don't always have to stay in those piles. In fact, particularly with one-patch or other overall patterns, using a fabric sometimes as a dark and sometimes as a medium, or another fabric sometimes as a light and sometimes as a medium, can make a project more interesting. The quilt can become rigid if all of the darks, mediums and lights are of equal value respectively. How a fabric "reads" in value is relative to what is next to it. Even though a fabric appears medium in tone, it can still serve as a dark as long as it is darker than those surrounding it.

Look again at the diagram for "Thousand Pyramids" (Diagram 4). The illustration looks stark because the darks are all very dark and the lights very light. With such contrast and equal amounts of light and dark, the eye has no resting place and it is not pleasing to look at the quilt for any length of time. The beauty of the "Thousand Pyramids" design is that through subtle shifts in shading overall larger triangular shapes begin to appear, giving an illusion of pyramids. The illusion is less apparent when there is a strong and consistent contrast between the lights

Diagram 7

and darks. Look now at Diagram 7. Larger pyramids can be seen, and the overall effect is generally more pleasing. Note that all of the lights are not very light, and all of the darks are not very dark. More medium tones have been used. Sometimes those mediums have been used as darks and sometimes as lights. Note the triangles that are of the same fabric, yet sometimes representing light and sometimes dark. Remember that any fabric can be fairly dark and yet still be used as a light as long as all the surrounding darks are darker.

The "Tumbling Blocks" pattern works much the same except that one needs contrasts between darks, mediums and lights, not just darks and lights, to get the pattern. Once again, the illustration in which the darks, mediums and lights are all of the same value is static (Diagram 5). It is much more interesting to make some of the lights darker, just so long as they are lighter than the darks and mediums surrounding them. The same goes for the darks and mediums. Don't always make them the same intensity. Study the example in Diagram 8 in which a

Diagram 8

variety of shadings have been used, and compare it to Diagram 5.

TEXTURE

The next area of concern in combining fabrics to create the scrap look is texture. By texture I don't mean the way a fabric <u>feels</u>, such as the differences between corduroy, satin and velvet, but rather the way it <u>looks</u>. The design on the fabric can create a look of texture. When working with many fabrics, try to find a wide variety of different small, medium and large prints. Using too many of the same type of print can create a monotonous or, depending on the prints, a busy look.

Once again when experimenting with different textures, you may find it easier to work first in black and white.

Color can influence a decision and if you learn to recognize textural differences in black and white, it will be easier to see them when you go to color. I actually photocopy fabrics; it makes it much easier to see only the print.

Try an experiment. Take the same group of fabrics that you sorted into dark, medium and light piles and now go over them for textural differences. See if you can find at least 12 fabrics with different textures. That means that you will have no two tiny florals, no two polka dots, etc. You might have a small pin dot, a small packed floral, a small more open viney floral, a large rose, a pin stripe, a border stripe and so on. Arrange them next to each other and then make your photocopy. Now check to see if the textures look as different in black and white as they do in color. You are apt to have a hard time finding as many as 12 different textures. The majority of the fabrics in quilt shops and the bulk of fabric in our own collections are small multi-colored floral prints. It is hard to find large print and striped fabrics, yet they are the very ones that can add a unique richness to a scrap look project.

See the fabric groups in Diagrams 9 and 10. The first one is uninteresting because all of the fabrics are too much the same, whereas the second one shows many different textures.

Of course, when working with many fabrics in a scrap quilt you will repeat texture types, but if you make sure to

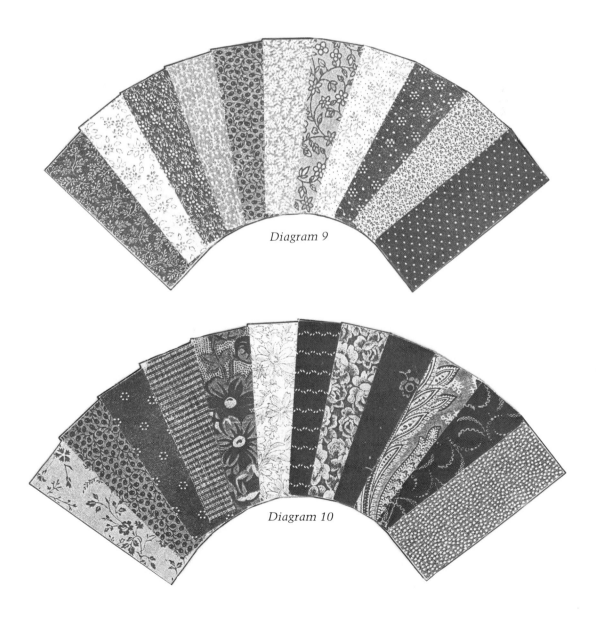

Diagram 9

Diagram 10

get as many different ones as you can, you will eliminate the monotony of too many similar fabrics.

Go back again to the diagrams of "Thousand Pyramids" (Diagrams 4 and 7) and "Tumbling Blocks" (Diagrams 5 and 8). The first versions (Diagrams 4 and 5) are too stark because they lack variety in the intensities of the darks, mediums and lights. The second versions (Diagrams 7 and 8) are better because the intensities vary, but they are also a bit monotonous because there is no textural difference in the fabrics. Now look at Diagrams 11 and 12 showing the same designs but with fabrics carefully selected with an eye to variety in prints as well as contrast. You can see graphically how textural differences enrich the designs!

Diagram 11

Diagram 12

COLOR

The use of color is difficult to teach. You can study the color wheel and various color theories, but in the end when you go to put the theories into practice, what you do boils down to instinct, how you feel about certain colors and your own likes and dislikes. By studying color you may try too hard to adhere to certain rules, and let your own sense of color go by the wayside. Listen to your heart, not to rules that others have made.

In this section on color all I can do is try to explain to you how I approach color and what seems to work best for me. I have never taken a class on color or studied the color wheel. I simply work with colors until they achieve a look that is pleasing to me. Often I am asked why I don't like bright or light colors. It is not that I don't like them, but that my own preference leans toward the darker, more muted shades. That does not mean that I don't admire lighter and brighter colors in someone else's work.

All quilters should work in colors they feel comfortable with and that they like to have around. Often, when teaching a class, I will look at the colors my students are wearing and then at the fabrics they are working with. Invariably the colors are the same. We tend to wear colors we like and use them in our homes and elsewhere. We should do the same in selecting colors for our quilts. By using the colors you like, that you feel comfortable with, you are apt to have greater success.

Bear in mind, then, that I'm not interested in telling you which colors to use, but only in suggesting ways to make the most of those you prefer.

Though a wide variety of shadings, colors and fabrics can be used effectively in a scrap look quilt, I try to adhere to some type of overall color scheme. I first decide what the main color or colors of the quilt will be, usually starting with two basic colors such as burgundy and blue, green and blue, brown and rust, red and green, or any other. If, for instance, I had decided upon brown and rust as the main colors, I would start by looking for many shadings of those two colors: from the lightest tans and beiges to the darkest cocoa browns, and in the rusts, from oranges and peaches to brick reds.

From that point I would add more colors—not completely new colors, but ones that are close to the basic choice. For instance, a burgundy would be in between a cocoa brown and the brick red and therefore not jump out as a completely different color, yet it would add a new dimension in shading. Once I had added burgundy, I might go to other shadings of burgundies from dusty pink and mauve to deep eggplant. I try not to let any color stand alone. In other words if you use blue, don't use it just once. Use various shadings of blue.

If you want to make something different from the traditional bright red and green Christmas quilt, try to use many shades of red and green, going from very dark tones to lighter and brighter ones. It is amazing how many different colors can be worked into a quilt as long as there is a shading from one color to the next. For instance, in my quilt, "Ode to Vasarely," (shown on the cover and in Color plate 3) I have used several shades of brown, rust, blue, orange, black, gray and burgundy. The colors blend because I have shaded from one color to the next. If the vivid blues and blacks were next to the oranges the effect would be jarring.

Jay Romano used many colors in her quilt, "Aurora." She had a sunrise in mind when she selected the fabrics, and through subtle shadings from one color to the next, she combined them effectively. (See Color plate 5.)

Sometimes, when working on the color scheme for a quilt, you may find that there are either too few colors or too many. You may not know what the problem is, but from looking at the quilt or fabrics you sense that something isn't right. When I planned "Castle Keep," my original color scheme was brown, rust, red and beige. The fabrics and colors seemed to look great together before I started, but after two blocks were pieced I realized that something was missing. They looked flat. fter experimenting with different fabrics, I finally decided to add green to some of the blocks and the problem was solved. The addition of the one extra color was all that was needed.

On the other hand, when I was piecing my charm quilt, "Aerial View," (Color plate 13) I tried to stick to soft shades of brown, rust, black, gray, burgundy, blue and green. That many colors seemed to be working well because they were so muted. However the more I looked at what I had pieced, the more I realized that something was wrong. It seemed that I had one color too many. In the end I removed all of the green pieces and was much more satisfied.

THE NEED FOR ACCENT AND DEEP DARK

There are two types of fabric that are essential to any color scheme. Both need to be used in small amounts and yet both enhance the impact of all the other colors. I call one the "accent" color and the other, the "deep dark" color.

The accent is a bright color that gives life to all the other colors. Such a spark has to be used sparingly or else it takes over. Someone said to me, "It's like the salt in the homemade ice cream. If there's too much it's terrible. If there's none it's bland." I always like the accent to be a brighter version of one of the colors I have already used. If my color scheme is blue and burgundy, the accent might be a brighter version of burgundy such as a dusty pink. It could also be a brighter blue. Orange might be the accent in a brown/rust combination. Once again shading is important. You would not want to stick a vivid orange in the middle of browns and rusts; you would make a transition to the orange with shades of rust. You must make sure the accent is related to other fabrics in the quilt so it does not stand alone. Orange was the color I used for the accent in "Ode to Vasarely" (Color plate 3). The orange is actually very bright, but because it is next to other rusts, the transition is subtle and the color does not jump out. Had I put one bright orange patch in the blue/black section of the quilt, it would have glared.

The deep dark fabric is just as important as the accent and must also, as I pointed out, be used sparingly or else the quilt will look too heavy. It should be a very dark version of one of the colors in the quilt. The fabric should be highly saturated with color and evoke a deep, rich feeling. In order for it to appear very dark, the fabric should not have much design in it. Any additional colors in the print may take away from the depth of color.

Black makes a good deep dark choice. (Notice its use in my two quilts, "Ode to Vasarely" and "Aerial View," Color plates 3 and 13.) People often shy away from using black in a quilt, but it can be very effective. If you have a brown/burgundy color scheme with some dark eggplants, adding a black as the very dark can be quite effective and it probably won't stand out at all. On the other hand, in a color scheme of pastels, a black fabric would be overwhelming. In a pastel setting the very dark fabric would be a lot lighter. At the risk of sounding like a broken record on relativity, I'll repeat myself: the depth of color in the deep dark fabric is all relative to the darkness of the other fabrics being used.

COMBINING CONTRAST, TEXTURE AND COLOR

It is not so difficult to deal with contrast, texture and color individually;

but to put the three together and to have to think of all of them at the same time can be much more challenging.

A good way to experiment with putting the three together is to try another exercise. Go back to the "Thousand Pyramids" design shown earlier (Diagrams 4, 7 and 11). Cut a triangle to use as a template. (There is a pattern in Diagram 102 if you need it.) Decide upon a color theme, gather a group of fabrics together, divide them into darks, mediums and lights, and check to make sure that you have a good variety in the types of prints.

Cut at least 20 different triangles from the fabrics and arrange them so that the darks are interspersed with the inverted lights making sure that the darks are not always very dark and the lights are not always very light. Be sure to mix in some mediums to add variety. At the same time that you are working with contrasts, be aware of the prints in the fabrics to be sure that compatible textures are next to each other. Too many large prints together can look very busy and too many small ones can be monotonous. Make sure there is a very dark fabric for depth and an accent for the spark.

If you have several triangles cut and arranged but are not satisfied with the way they look, you may have come up against a common problem. There are some other types of fabrics that I haven't mentioned yet that I try to avoid. These are what I call "busy prints." I make three classifications of busy prints.

One type is the small print with more than two colors. By two colors, I mean shades of one color as well as two different colors. In other words, I consider a tan and dark brown fabric a two color print. If the fabric has one or more additional colors I usually do not use it in my work. This happens to be my personal preference, based on lots of trial and error. In my own work I have found that the colors in small-scale, multi-print fabrics bleed into the adjoining fabrics creating a loss of clear definition of the shape of the pieces. I want to emphasize, however, that it is only with <u>small</u> prints that I adhere to my two color rule. With larger prints and stripes I often choose fabrics that have multiple colors.

The examples in Diagram 13 show some multi-color small print fabrics. Even in black and white they appear busy.

A second type of what I call busy

Diagram 13

1. Eight-pointed Star. 105″ x 105″. Pieced stars of multiple fabrics with broderie perse appliquéd flowers. On the back of the quilt is written "Presented to Ann Elizabeth Ayers by her mother Jany 1867 made and quilted by her Grandma Bonsall in 1830." From the collection of Diana Leone.

2. Hexagon Diamonds. Ca. 1830. 88″ x 97″. Many different fabrics have been used in this variation of the hexagon, yet they have been organized to give a unifying effect. Author's collection.

3. Ode to Vasarely. 72″ x 84″. Made by author. Begun in 1980 and completed in 1985, this quilt was inspired by a postcard showing one of Victor Vasarely's paintings.

5. Aurora. 30″ x 36″. Charm quilt made by Jay Romano in 1985, using 300 triangles —all of different fabrics.

4. Francly Radiant. 58″ x 58″. Made by Linda Pool in 1985.

6, 7. Big Red. 72″ x 66″. Made by Fay Goldey in 1984, from 564 different red fabrics. **Evening Star**, (right) has more than 40 fabrics. 66″ x 94″. By Susan Powers, 1984.

8. Castle Keep. 75″ x 96″. Made by author in 1981. Many different fabrics have been used in this quilt, but care was taken to keep similar colors in the same areas of the block.

9, 10. Pandemonium. 72″ x 86″. Charm quilt top of 999 different fabrics, made by Lenore Parham in 1985. **Valley Star**. 32″ x 42″. Made by Barbara Bockman in 1984. Some fabrics have been embellished with stenciling.

11, 12. Metro. 43″ x 43″. Made by Judy Spahn in 1984. **Ocean Waves**, (right). 72″ x 72″. Ca. 1900. From the collection of Dick and Ellen Swanson.

13, 14. Aerial View. 72″ x 91″.
Made by author in 1985. With the
exception of the border, this
charm quilt top has 925 pieces, all
of different fabrics. Detail shows
effect of using prints of different
scale.

15, 16, 17. Streak of Lightning, (at left). Ca. 1870. 83″ x 88″. Charm quilt of 997 different fabrics. **Concentric Triangles**. Ca. 1880, from Lehigh County, Pa., 77″ x 84″. Charm quilt of 888 different fabrics, including some centennial fabrics. Both from author's collection. **Triangles**. Ca. 1870 from Pennsylvania. 90″ x 94″. The placement of the 460 different triangles in this charm quilt produces a "barn-raising" type pattern. Dick and Ellen Swanson collection.

18, 19. Thousand Pyramids. Ca. 1870. 88″ x 93″. There are 1,066 different pieces in this charm quilt. Throughout the quilt it appears as though identical fabrics were put side by side deliberately, but closer examination reveals ever so slight differences in color or pattern (see detail). Author's collection.

20, 21. Hexagon Charm Quilt. Ca. 1875. 79″ x 91″. Charm quilt with 488 different pieces. Of special interest (shown in detail) are the striped fabrics, all going in the same direction. Author's collection.

prints are those with a strong contrast between light and dark, especially white (or very light) with a dark color (Diagram 14). These types of fabrics tend to jump out and call attention to themselves interfering with a smooth blending of prints. Of course, the amount of white will make a difference as to whether or not the print appears busy. For instance, a tiny pin dot fabric will not appear busy, whereas a fabric with larger polka dots will (Diagram 15).

The fabrics in Diagram 16 offer interesting examples of a busy and a nonbusy print. A fabric salesman showed me a swatch of the fabric on the left. I liked it and ordered some in several col-

ors. When the fabric arrived it was the print on the right. I didn't like it at all and knew I never would have ordered it. I called the company and was told that the dots in the first sample were so small that during the printing process many were filling up with dye. They solved the problem by enlarging the design. The two designs are the same all right, but the one with the larger dots looks busy.

The third type of print I consider busy is a two color print which has equal amounts of the two colors. This type is harder to pick out and define; it sneaks up on you. I have sometimes purchased a fabric that I thought was

Diagram 14

Diagram 15

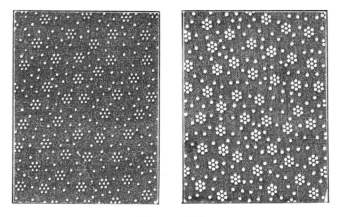

Diagram 16

wonderful, only to discover when I tried using it that it just didn't work. The fabric didn't fit into my two other classifications of busy prints and yet it didn't work with other prints. I finally realized what was wrong with it: the colors in the fabric were almost exactly equal. If you go back to the "Thousand Pyramids" (Diagram 4) you will notice that because there are equal amounts of light and dark it is less pleasing to look at than Diagram 11. Likewise when there are equal amounts of two colors within one print your eye jumps back

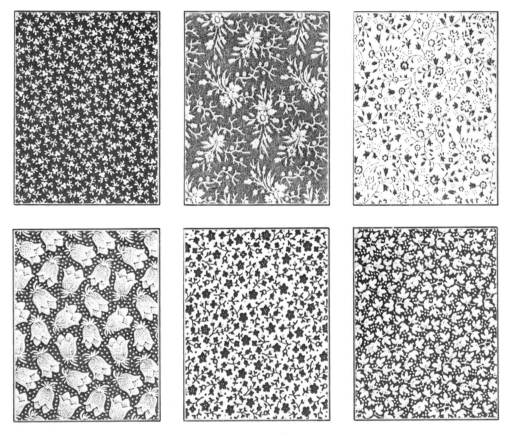

Diagram 17

and forth between the two looking for a resting place. There are several examples shown in Diagram 17. For the same reason "op art" designs are hard to look at for any length of time.

Look at the two cabbage rose prints in Diagram 18. The prints are almost identical, yet the first appears busy and the second does not. With the first print there is a stronger contrast between light and dark and also equal amounts of the two colors. In the fabric on the right there is more light than dark (giving the eye a place to rest) as well as a

Diagram 18

more subtle contrast between the two colors.

Look now at the two illustrations of the triangles below (Diagram 19). The one on the left is a pleasing blend of fabrics. When only two busy prints are added as in the illustration on the right, the overall balance is lost. There are 16 triangles in the illustration and two busy prints have spoiled the whole effect. The other 14 no longer work as harmoniously as they did. Your eye

Diagram 19

jumps immediately to the busy prints and misses seeing the fabrics as a whole.

Now go back to the fabric triangles you cut out and see if there are any of the fabrics that I have described as busy. If there are, cut more triangles from non-busy fabrics and lay them on top. See if it makes a difference in the overall look.

If you find you have too many busy fabrics in your stash, don't despair. There are uses for them. Many busy prints work much better with solid colored fabrics which tend to calm them down.

Notice how busy prints look with other busy prints in the 9-patch designs (on the left in Diagram 20) and how

they look with solids (the two versions on the right). The busier prints look better with the solid colors. If your goal is to use mostly prints in your quilt, you will achieve a better effect by eliminating the "busys."

Prints that are busy because of too sharp a contrast can be salvaged sometimes by toning down the light areas with a dip in a commercial fabric dye or a soak in a strong solution of hot tea as previously described.

By doing the simple exercises described here and by staying aware of the need to keep a proper balance between contrast, textures and color, you will be well on your way toward creating your very own scrap look quilt.

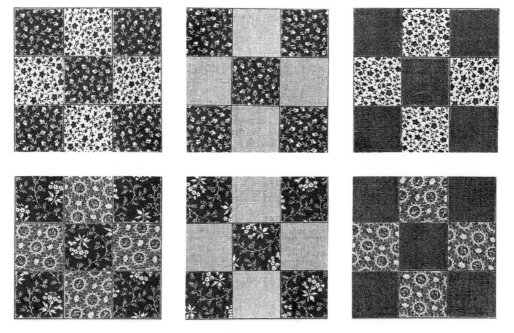

Diagram 20

One-Patch Multi-Fabric Quilts

The term "one-patch" refers to a quilt design in which there is a single geometric shape that is repeated throughout the quilt, most commonly a square, a triangle, a hexagon or a diamond. Many other shapes are also used, and the variety of designs which can be achieved with any of the one-patches is endless.

PIECING THE ONE-PATCH

Once the design has been chosen, the dark, medium, light contrast decided upon, and the fabrics selected, the next most important task is deciding on a workable unit for piecing the design. With overall one-patch quilts one is tempted to start at one end of the quilt and piece it in rows, or alternatively to spread out all the pieces (on the floor or tacked to a wall) and decide how they should all go before any of the piecing has begun.

When making a scrapbag quilt in which you want to use as many different fabrics as possible, the chances of having all the fabrics on hand that will ultimately be used are slim. Once the quilt has been started it is more than likely that you will continue to haunt fabric stores and friends' fabric collections looking for more pieces.

By starting the piecing at one end of the quilt and sewing the rows together as you go, it will be difficult to add new fabrics to the finished part of the quilt. You may not be able to keep the colors and fabric types in balance. Also, the type of colors and fabrics selected on any given day may reflect your mood at that time. If it is a dark, dreary day and you are in a bad mood, the color and fabric section sewn on that day may be dreary and dull. On the other hand, if you are in a good mood and it is cheerful and bright outside, the piecing may take on a more open, airy feeling.

With all this in mind, you can see why I believe the best approach is to find a unit for piecing. Study the overall design of the quilt and try to discover a way to break it down into units so that when the units are placed side by side, the overall design of the quilt will remain intact. For example, one might divide the "Thousand Pyramids" design, which has been discussed earlier, into two alternating units as in Diagram 21. One unit is pieced with

Diagram 21

the dark triangles at the base pointing upward and the other with the light triangles pointing upward.

When the units are put together they are alternated with the dark triangles pointing up and the light ones pointing down. (Diagram 22).

Diagram 22

Rather than worry about color and fabric placement in the overall quilt, I concern myself first with the individual units. I try to make every unit pleasing, concentrating in each one on a proper blending of contrasts, textures and colors. In a quilt such as "Ode to Vasarely," shown in Color plate 3 (see piecing unit that was used in Diagram

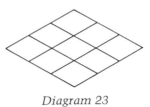

Diagram 23

23) where I know that I will want shading from one color to another, I plan some units of specific colors. In that quilt there are units which are basically brown or rust, others which are mostly blue and some which are blendings from brown to rust, and so on. I had no master plan before I started as to overall color arrangement. My only plan was for the arrangement of the geometric shapes. It is only after all the units of a quilt are pieced that I spread them out and plan the color arrangement. For me it is much easier to work on the final plan after the units are complete, moving and changing them until I find the placement that is most satisfying. Sometimes, in order to achieve specific effects, I will have to piece additional units of certain colors.

Piecing in units this way allows greater flexibility in the use of colors, contrasts and textures throughout the whole quilt. If you find a wonderful new fabric or color towards the end of the project when most of the units are pieced, you can put that fabric into all of the remaining units. Then, when the units are arranged for the layout of the quilt, they can be spread throughout so that they are not concentrated in one area.

By piecing in units and occasionally spreading them out to get a feeling for what the quilt looks like, you also can make corrections along the way. For instance, one time when I laid out the units of "Ode to Vasarely" I got a heavy, overwhelming black feeling. Instead of replacing some of the black, I simply refrained from using any more black in the quilt. That way the black that I had already used was able to be dispersed evenly throughout the quilt. Another time when I spread out the units, I had a feeling of too many small prints. With all the fabrics appearing too similar to each other, the quilt was becoming monotonous. I found some fabrics with larger textures and pieced several units concentrating on using the larger prints, and the next time I spread them out the whole effect had changed.

ONE-PATCH DESIGNS

One-patch designs are like mosaics of tiles. Each patch connects to the next and, depending on the colors and fabrics used, can create a myriad of designs. In this section on one-patch designs I will show some of the more common shapes along with unusual ways in which many of them can be put together. For each design I give a pattern in several sizes.

One-patch designs are unique in that you usually do not need to add seam allowances to the pieces in order to make the shapes fit together. In designs that have several different pattern pieces the pattern cannot be enlarged or reduced by adding or taking away equal amounts from all sides of all pieces. The pattern must be redrafted in order for the pattern pieces to fit together properly. To enlarge or reduce one-patch designs, however, in which all pieces in

the quilt are the same, you only need to add or take away equal amounts to all sides of the template.

It is very important, however, to realize that the proportions of some shapes will change when you add or take away equal amounts from all sides. Look at two illustrations of the hexagon and the half hexagon (Diagram 24). The heavy

Diagram 24

line indicates the original shape. As equal amounts are added or taken away from the hexagon, the shape always remains the same proportions. However, the half hexagon changes. As the shape gets larger or smaller it is no longer a perfect half of a hexagon.

I tried to figure out why some shapes could have equal amounts added to or taken away from all sides without changing the proportions and others could not. A square works, a rectangle does not. So I thought the shape must have to have equal sides and equal angles. But any triangle or diamond works and they don't all have equal sides and angles. I finally got the answer from Lesly-Claire Greenberg.

She said that if you could fit a circle inside the shape with the circle touching all sides, then you could add or take away equal amounts from the sides of the shape without changing the proportion. All other shapes require redrafting in order for the proportions to remain the same. The illustrations in Diagram 25 show some shapes and how a circle

plate with the quarter inch added.

All patterns given here that are not nested into each other with quarter-inch margins at each side cannot have equal amounts added to the sides without changing the shape. Select the size you want for the finished piece and add your own seam allowance.

Most of the designs in this chapter

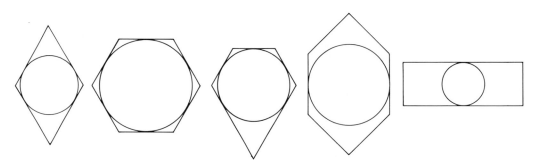

Diagram 25

would or would not fit inside of them. The three shapes at the left could have equal amounts added to or taken away from all sides without changing the proportions of the shape. The two shapes at the right could not.

The patterns for one-patch designs given here have been treated in two ways. Those in which equal amounts can be added or taken away from all sides without changing the shape have been nested into each other in quarter-inch increments. Select the pattern you want for the finished piece and then go to the next larger size to get the template.

have been shown in dark, medium and light shadings. By adhering to the guidelines set down in the previous chapter on contrast, texture and color, any of them can take on the scrap look.

Designs Based on the Hexagon

Designs based on the hexagon are probably the most common of all one-patch patterns. In addition to the basic hexagon as used in the "Grandmother's Flower Garden" or in the overall mosaic pattern, the hexagon broken in half or into diamonds or triangles is the basis for many other designs.

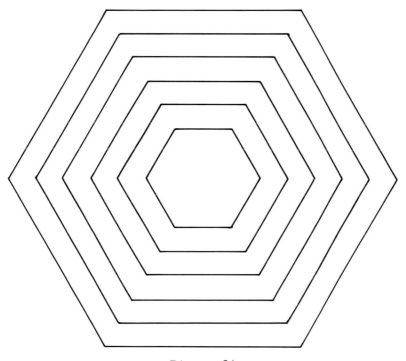

Diagram 26

Basic Hexagon

There are as many ways to design with the basic hexagon as there are ideas. I have seen baskets, flowers, even people created in mosaic form depending upon the placement of the colors in the various hexagons. If you would like to experiment, put a piece of tissue

Diagram 27

paper over the page of hexagons (Diagram 27) and start coloring. Photographs 2 and 22 and Color plates 2, 20 and 21 show quilts using the hexagon.

Some of the more traditional ways of putting hexagons together are shown in Diagrams 28–32. Color plate 2 shows a beautiful antique quilt composed of hexagons. Photograph 2 shows how carefully the hexagons were cut with flowers centered in the middle of each one.

Diagram 30

Diagram 28

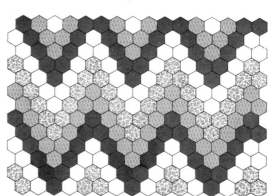

Diagram 31

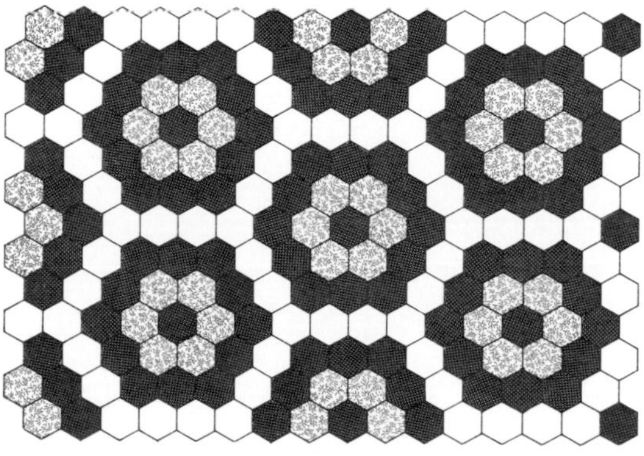

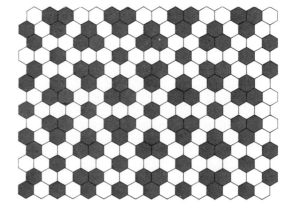

Diagram 29

Diagram 32

2. Hexagon Diamond. Detail of Color plate 2. Notice how care has been taken to center motifs from the fabric in each hexagon.

Half Hexagon

The half hexagon is the shape I used to create a quilt I call "Inner City" (see Diagram 36). I had thought it was an original design until I found several references to it. The earliest mention is in the *Dictionary of Needlework*, 1882, where it is incorrectly called "Right Angle Patchwork." In studying the fabrics in the quilt in Photograph 1, I discovered a fabric with the same design. This quilt dates back at least to 1880 (Diagram 35).

The sewing unit used for "Inner City" is the Y-shaped piece shown in

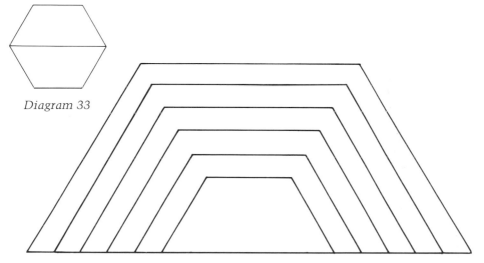

Diagram 33

Diagram 34

Diagram 35

Diagram 36

Diagram 37. All of the individual units were pieced and then I experimented with various ways of laying them out until I found an arrangement I liked.

Below are some other design possibilities using the half hexagon. In each of these designs I would probably sew the pieces together in rows or half rows and then wait until all individual rows were sewn to put them together.

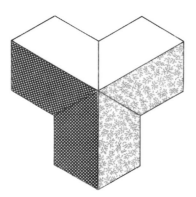

Diagram 37

Diagram 39

Diagram 38

Diagram 40

The 60° Diamond

The 60° diamond which can be drafted from the hexagon, (see Diagram 41) is one of my favorite shapes to work with. It is the shape I used in my charm quilt, "Aerial View," (Color plates 13 and 14) and in "Ode to Vasarely," (Color plate 3). The most common design made from this shape is the familiar pattern "Tumbling Blocks" (see Photo-

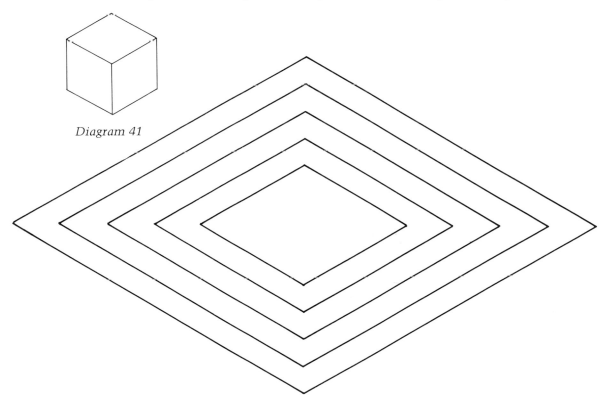

Diagram 41

Diagram 42

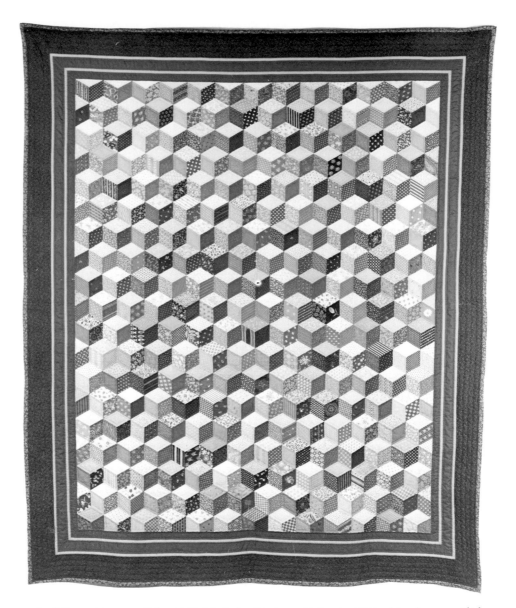

3. Building a Dream. 87″ x 103″. Made by Kathryn Kuhn in 1984, this charm quilt has 750 different fabrics. The colors are black, green and purple.

graph 3). Diagram 43 shows the piecing unit, composed of 12 diamonds, I use when sewing that design. As long as care is taken to keep all the units going in the same direction, the tumbling block pattern will be created when the units are placed side by side. The heavy dark line in Diagram 44 outlines one of the piecing units.

In the next version of the diamond,

known as "The Columbia," the piecing unit is the same hexagon with 12 diamonds as above, but the light and dark placement is different. In this case a six-pointed star is pieced of dark and medium diamonds, and the hexagon is filled in with light colored diamonds (Diagram 45). When the units are put

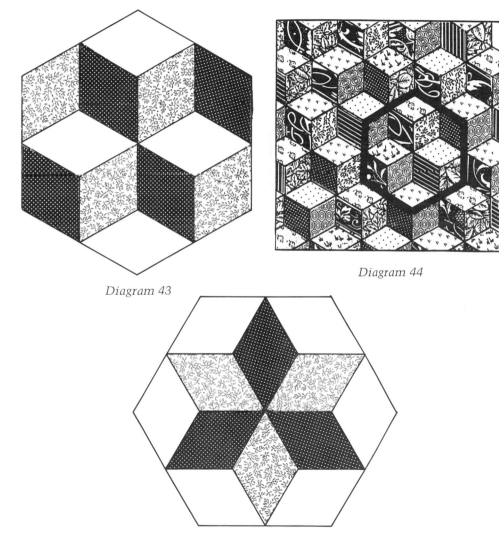

Diagram 43

Diagram 44

Diagram 45

4. The Columbia. Ca. 1920. 70″ x 72″. Consistency has been used in the placement of lights and darks in this multi-fabric quilt.

together you see stars as well as light colored blocks. (See Photograph 4.) The heavy line in Diagram 46 indicates one of the piecing units.

Intrigued with the blocks and stars evident in Photograph 4, I decided to study other ways of putting the diamonds together to achieve the effect of

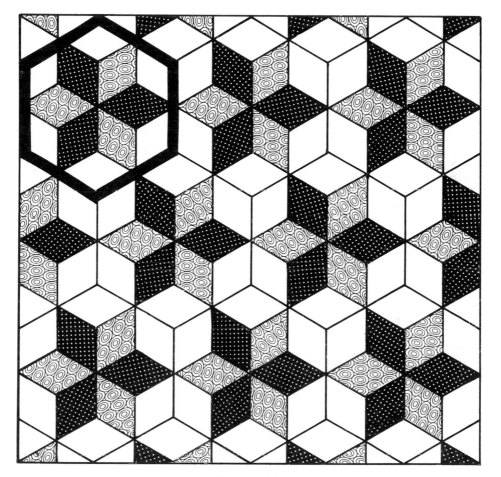

Diagram 46

blocks as well as stars. I had been told that in order for the tumbling blocks to show up, one always needed to have dark on one side, medium on another and light on the third. When someone tells me that something must be done a certain way, I usually feel compelled to try to do it differently. I began working

Diagram 47

with the design and came up with the version in Diagram 47.

Sometimes the stars are evident and sometimes the blocks. If you pick out any one dark patch you will see that it has only medium and light patches next to it. Every light patch has only dark and mediums next to it. Keeping all of that straight may seem mind-boggling, but it is relatively easy. There are three piecing units—still the same hex-agon with 12 diamonds as above—but each unit is different in terms of the light and dark placement. In the first unit the star is pieced with dark and medium diamonds and the hexagon is filled in with light diamonds. In the second, the star is pieced with dark and light diamonds with mediums around the edge; in the last the star is pieced of light and mediums with dark around the edge (Diagram 48).

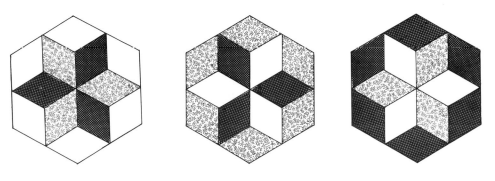

Diagram 48

To put the units together, piece them in rows alternating dark, medium and light in each row as shown in Diagram 49. The illustration outlines the various units.

Several years ago a friend sent me a

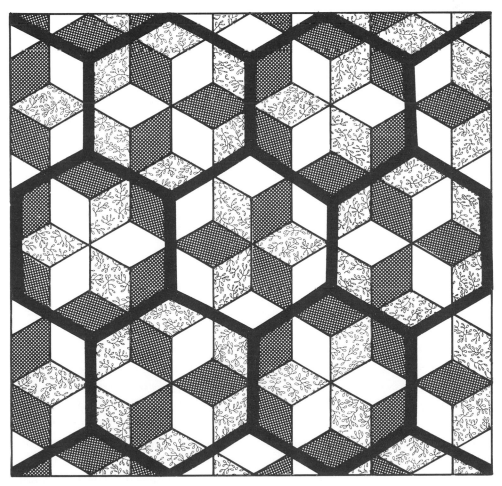

Diagram 49

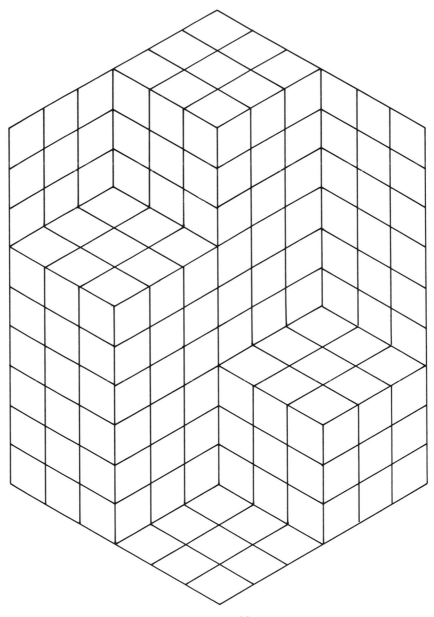

Diagram 50

picture postcard of a painting by Victor Vasarely, in which he had taken several large diamonds and fragmented them with smaller diamonds. The basic layout of the diamonds he used is shown in Diagram 50.

I was intrigued by his design, not only because it was a takeoff on the basic tumbling block pattern which I had always loved, but also because I liked the idea of breaking down the larger diamonds and getting more chance to play around with shadings of color.

After working with the idea for several months I designed my quilt (Color plate 3), which I named "Ode to Vasarely" out of gratitude for his inspiration. I used four of his units, but reversed two and overlapped them and then filled in the edges to square off the design. That gave me the basic layout of my quilt. From that point on I pieced individual diamond units (shown in Diagram 51), experimenting with shad-

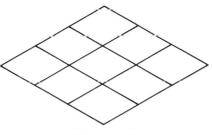

Diagram 51

ings and colors until I had enough units for the quilt. I shaded the units with lights to darks going from end to end on some and from side to side on others. When I put them all on a wall to decide upon final placement, I discovered I had to discard some units and piece a few new ones in order to achieve the effect I wanted.

Quilters have various methods of putting their work on a wall. Some use a giant cork board; others pin directly into the wall. I used to pin to my grass cloth wallpaper. At any rate it is much better to look at the work from a distance when it is on the wall than when it's on the floor.

The design in "Aerial View," shown in Color plate 13, was a further experiment with the layout of the diamonds I had used in "Ode to Vasarely." The unit I used for piecing is shown in Diagram 52. Half the units were pieced exactly like it, and the other half were mirror images of it. Two opposite quarter sections of the quilt use the same units. By being consistent with the dark, medium and light placement, blocks looking like buildings show up as well as a secondary design. (Diagram 53)

The next version of using the diamond can either be pieced in the larger

Diagram 52

Diagram 53

hexagon units as outlined in Diagram
54 or in the smaller diamond unit
placed next to it (Diagram 55).

Diagram 54

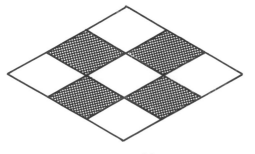

Diagram 55

Below are more diagrams (Diagrams 56-63) showing other ways to arrange 60° diamond pieces. Those which have several possibilities for shading have been left uncolored so that you can study them and choose your own arrangement.

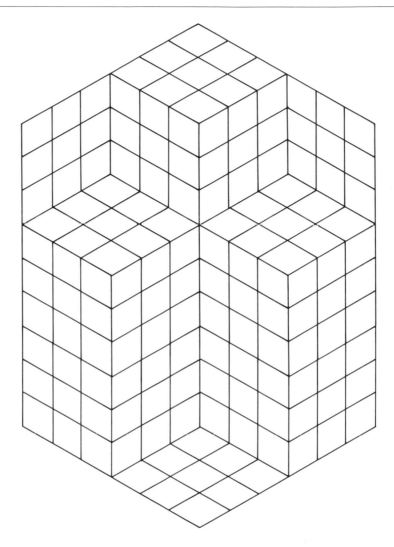

Diagram 56

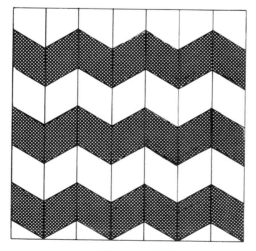

Diagram 57   *Diagram 58*

Diagram 59

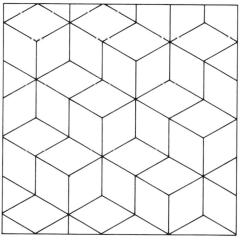

Diagram 60

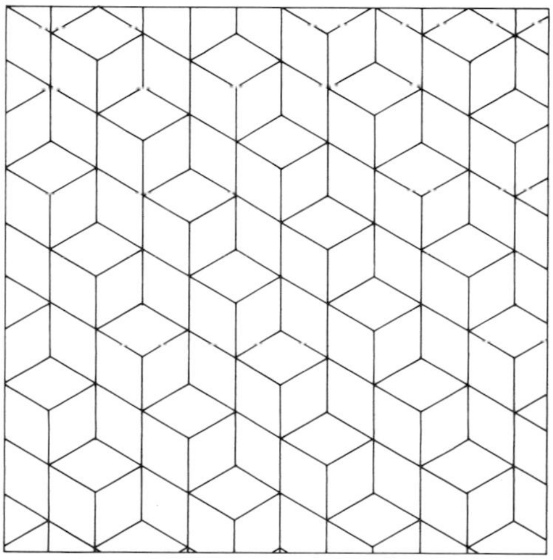

Diagram 61

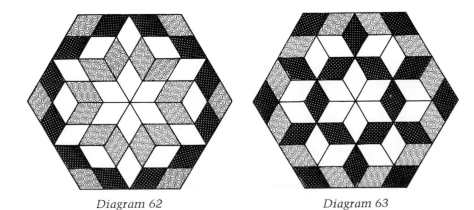

Diagram 62

Diagram 63

Equilateral Triangle

If the diamond shown in the previous designs is cut in half crosswise (see Diagram 64) it produces a triangle from which many designs can also be made. This triangle is often used in the "Thousand Pyramids" design, but that pattern also uses a taller, thinner triangle (see Diagram 102). The quilts shown in Photographs 26 and 27 and Color plates 16, 18 and 19 have the equilateral triangle as the pattern.

Another way of putting the triangles

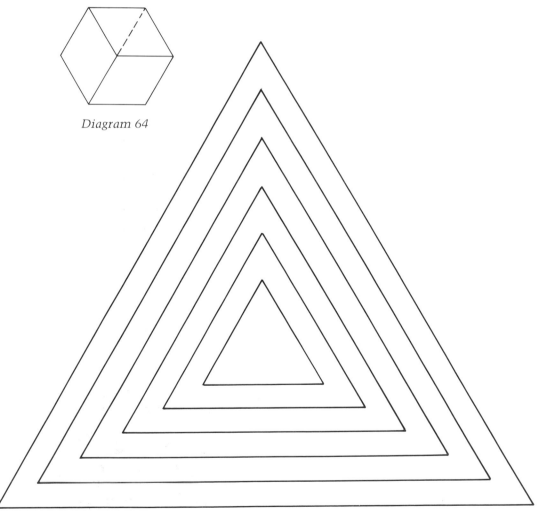

Diagram 64

Diagram 65

together is shown in Diagram 66. This version is graphically interesting because sometimes light stars are seen, sometimes dark ones and at other times medium ones. Individual hexagons may also be seen. To piece this version, make a hexagon shaped unit composed of six triangles. Two triangles are dark, two are medium and the other two are light. When you sew the units together, take care not to have any two dark, light or medium triangles next to each other. The dark line outlines the piecing unit in the diagram.

Diagram 66

Other Shapes Based On the Hexagon

The 60° diamond can also be split lengthwise (see Diagram 67) to achieve an interesting shape for a one-patch quilt. Diagram 69 shows one of the design possibilities using this shape.

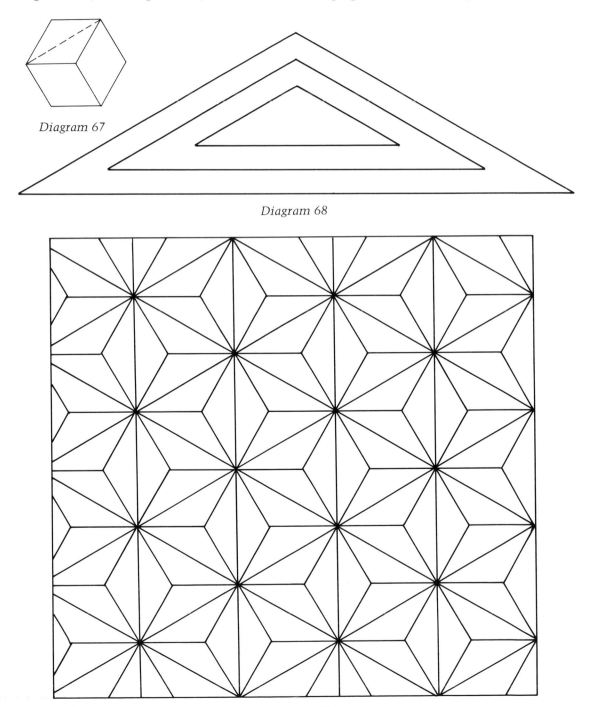

Diagram 67

Diagram 68

Diagram 69

The next shape is also based on a hexagon. Diagram 70 shows how the hexagon is broken down to achieve the shape and Diagram 71 gives templates. Fay Goldey used this template to create her quilt "Big Red" shown in Color plate 6.

The first version of the design is the traditional way of putting it together called "Colonial Garden." In this variation the shading is basically lights and darks.

The shapes can also be put together in the style of the "Thousand Pyra-

Diagram 70

Diagram 71

mids" design alternating lights and darks, but with the addition of mediums for interest (Diagram 73).

In the last version lights, mediums and darks are necessary to get the design. A heavy line indicates where the piecing unit is.

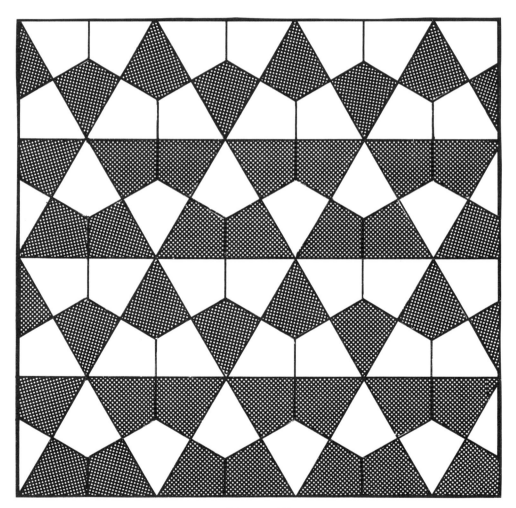

Diagram 72

Diagram 73

Diagram 74

This next one-patch shape is based on a version of the hexagon I saw in the March 1980 issue of *Quilter's Newsletter Magazine*. It makes an interesting allover pattern. Diagram 75 again shows how the hexagon is broken down.

I want to end this group of one-patch

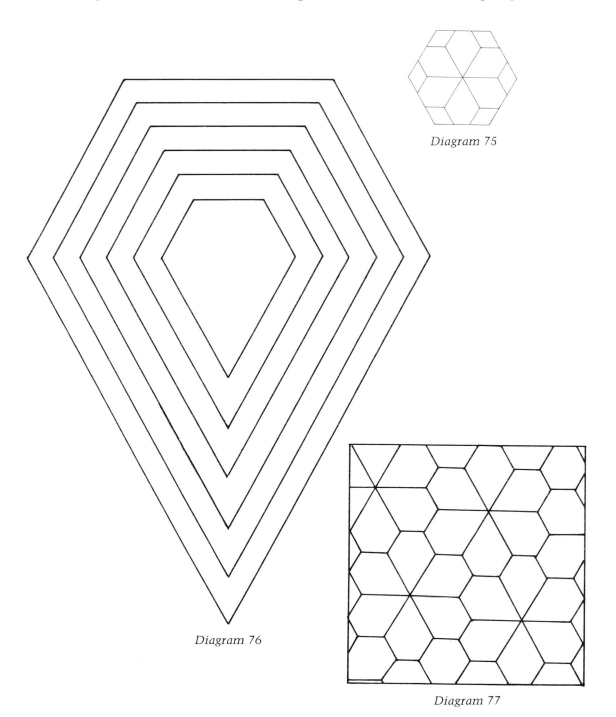

Diagram 75

Diagram 76

Diagram 77

shapes based on hexagons with one of my original designs. I call the design "3-D" because it reminds me of the many sided dice that my son uses in his "Dungeons and Dragons" game. Diagram 78 shows how the shape appears within the hexagon.

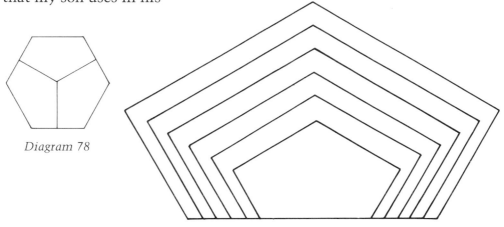

Diagram 78

Diagram 79

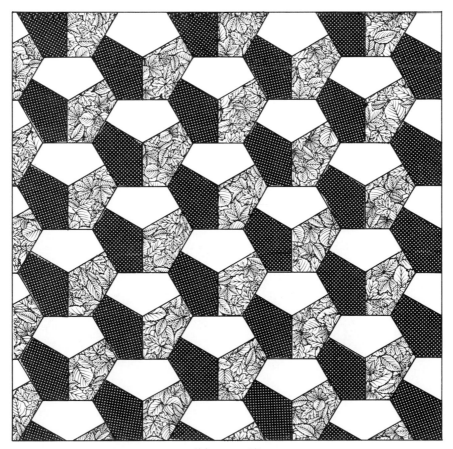

Diagram 80

Square

The possibilities of designing with the square are endless. One can do mosaics, scenes, very graphic configurations, you name it. The four-patch and the nine-patch (Diagrams 82 and 83) are the most basic designs using the square.

If individual four-patch blocks are put together, a simple checkerboard is the result unless care is taken to alter the coloring in some way to give a different effect.

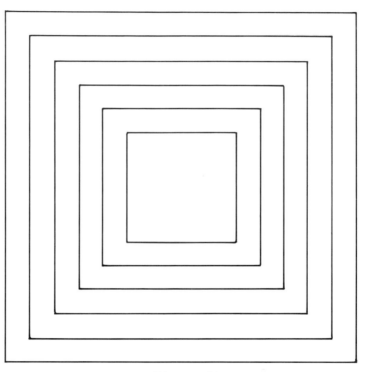

Diagram 81

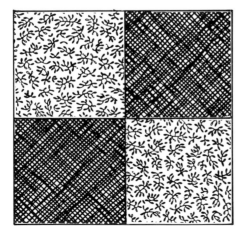

Diagram 82

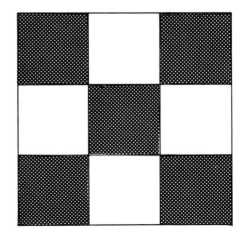

Diagram 83

5. Magellan's Charm. 72" x 72". Made by Kathryn Kuhn in 1984, this quilt is in brown, rust, black and green. It has 877 different fabrics.

The quilt, "Magellan's Charm," in Photographs 5 and 6, shows the "Trip Around the World" version of putting together squares. This quilt was made by Kathryn Kuhn and is a charm quilt in which no two fabrics are alike.

The basic nine-patch can be very appealing by itself as is evident in the pair of pillow cases shown here (Photograph 7). These have been made with a variety of different fabrics. Each nine-patch square has been alternated with a plain white square.

The quilt in Photograph 8 is simply a series of tiny nine-patch blocks put together, but the maker had a plan to create the overall design. The quilt is pieced in large squares. Each large square is broken down into nine small nine-patch squares. (See the detail in Photograph 9.) When all of the large squares are sewn together they form the overall design.

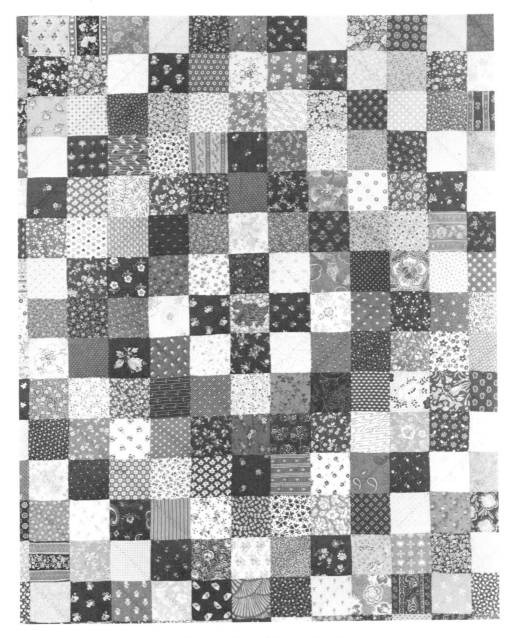

6. **Magellan's Charm**. Detail.

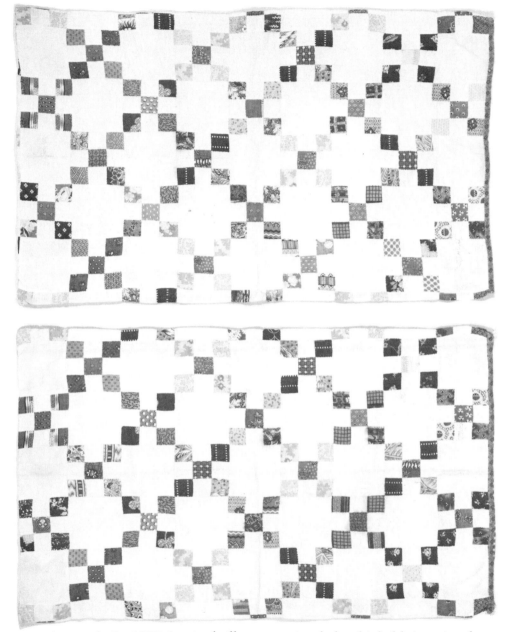

7. Nine-patch. Ca. 1870. A pair of pillow cases pieced of multiple fabrics using the nine-patch pattern. From the collection of Dick and Ellen Swanson.

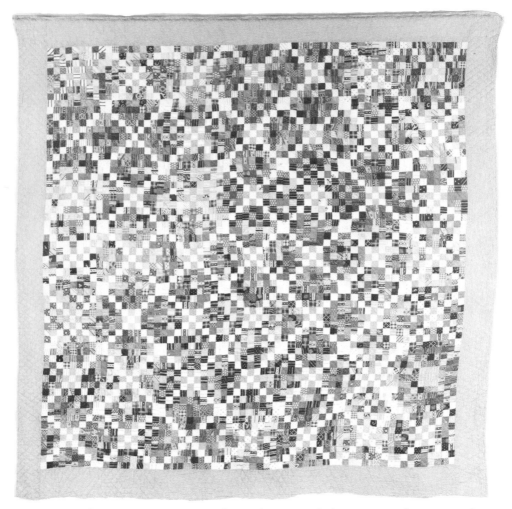

8. Nine-patch. Ca. 1880. 80″ x 84″. This quilt is pieced of tiny one-inch squares. The colors are predominantly browns and pinks.

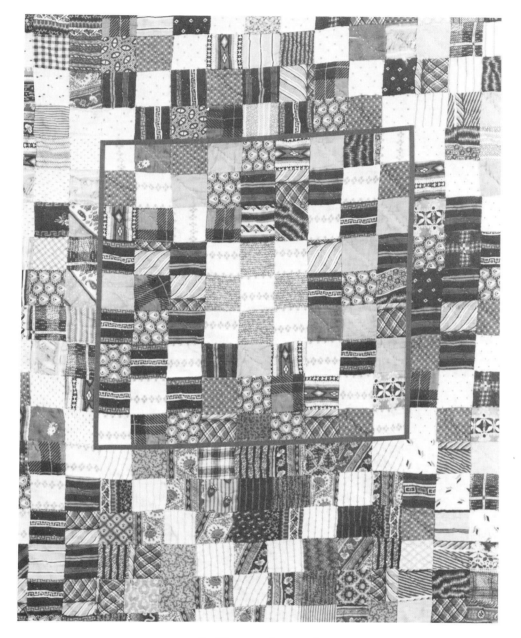

9. Nine-patch. Detail.

Rectangle

Many interesting one-patch designs employ the rectangle as the pattern piece. Two shapes of rectangles are most commonly used: the first divides a square in half lengthwise (Diagram 84) and the other divides the square lengthwise into thirds (Diagram 86).

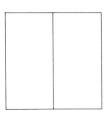

Diagram 84

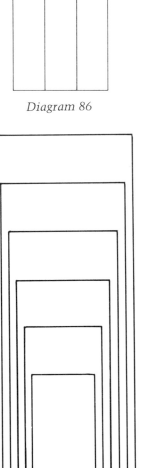

Diagram 86

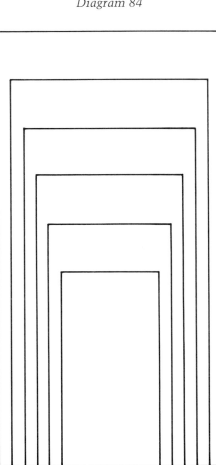

Diagram 85

Diagram 87

10. Brickwork. Ca. 1910. 84″ x 90″. A quilt top pieced of multiple fabrics in blue, white, red and burgundy, the consistent use of contrast and color makes an appealing visual impact. Author's collection.

Photographs 10 and 11 show two quilts using the "Brickwork" pattern. Even though both are of the same design, they look very different because the first one uses four large squares, whereas the second uses only one square of the design and builds outward from the center. Color plate 15 shows

11. Rail Fence Variation. Ca. 1910. 81″ x 89″. Quilt top pieced in red, burgundy, white and blue rectangles. Author's collection.

another quilt which uses a rectangle for its template. In that quilt the rectangles are arranged in a pattern known as "Streak of Lightning." In these three quilts the rectangle is made from dividing a square in half.

The following illustrations (Diagrams 88–91) show other design variations using the rectangle.

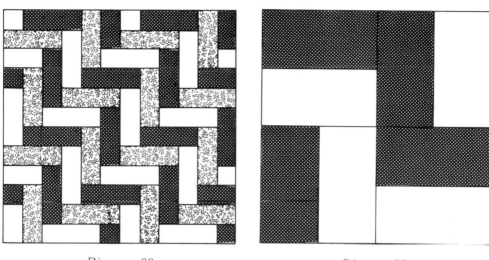

Diagram 88

Diagram 89

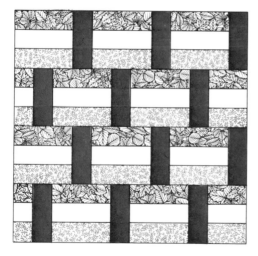

Diagram 90

Diagram 91

The Right Angle Triangle

The 90° triangle is a versatile shape and there are many ways of designing with it to create an overall one-patch quilt. The quilts shown in Color plates 5, 9 and 12 all use this shape as the pattern. A few other variations are shown in Diagrams 93-98.

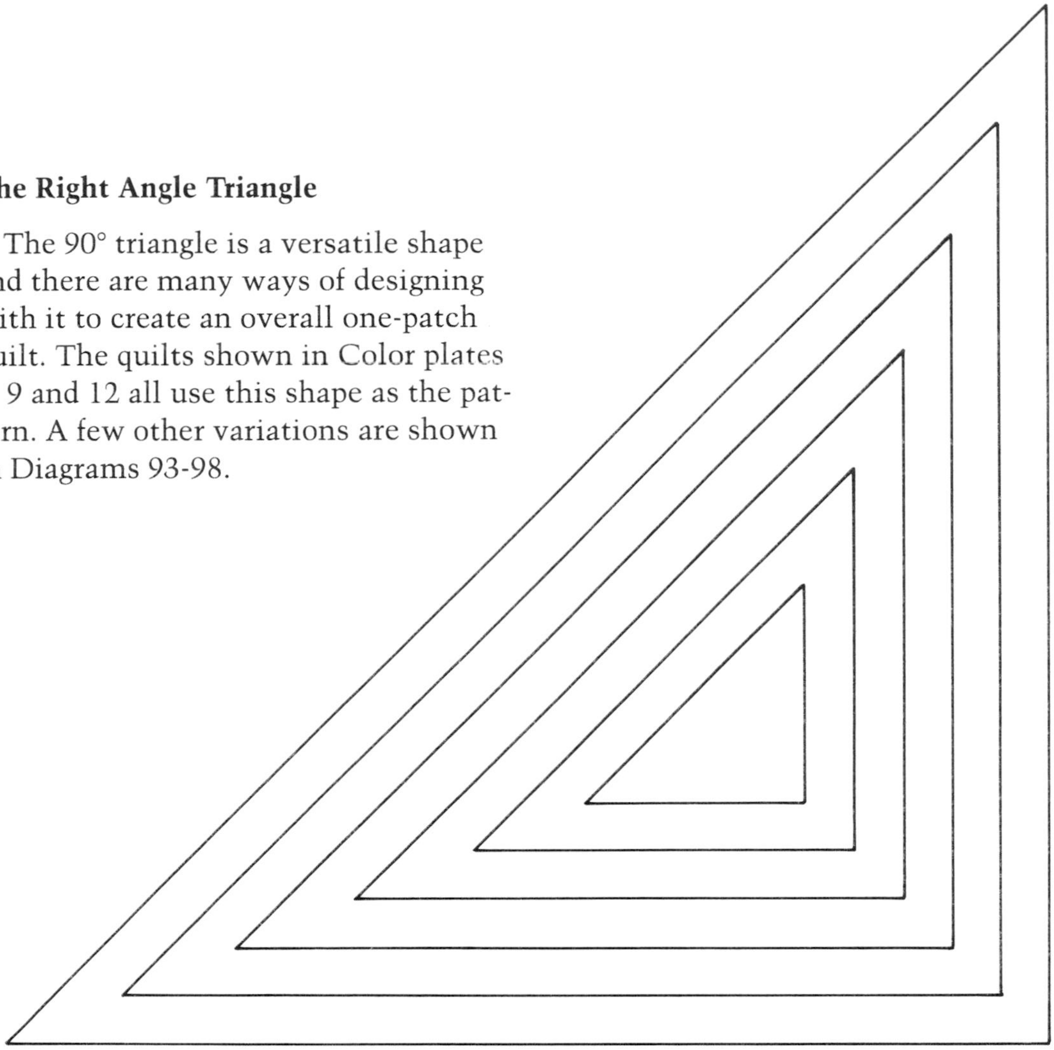

Diagram 92

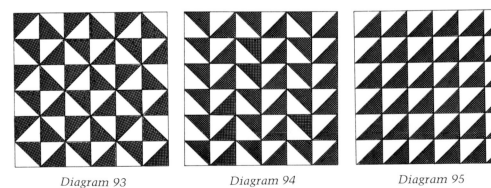

Diagram 93   *Diagram 94*   *Diagram 95*

Diagram 96

Diagram 97

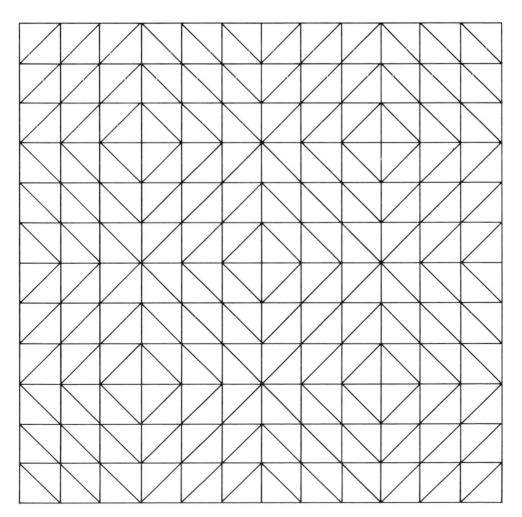

Diagram 98

The 45° Diamond

The 45° diamond has been used frequently as an allover pattern similar to
the "Lone Star."

If the diamond is cut in half lengthwise a completely different allover
effect can be achieved as shown in Diagram 101. Notice the optical illusion.
At first glance one thinks that the verti-
cal and horizontal lines cutting through
the middle of the diagram are tapered
towards the center. But if you put a
ruler on the lines you will see that they
are perfectly straight.

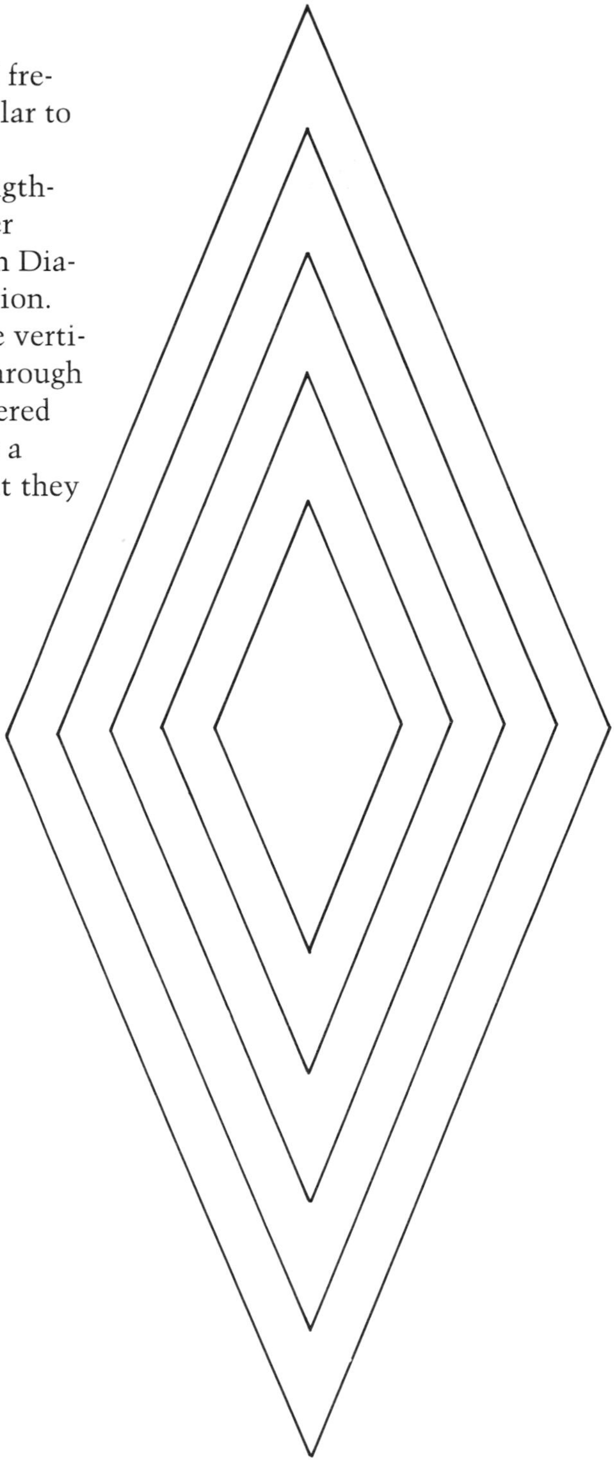

Diagram 99

Diagram 100

Diagram 101

Odd Shapes
For Creating One-Patch Quilts

There are many other shapes that can be used for creating one-patch quilts. Several are shown here, along with some design possibilities for their use. By varying the fabric, color and contrasts within the designs many unusual adaptations can be achieved.

Thousand Pyramids

This design has been discussed in detail earlier, but here is a pattern in case you would like to try your own version.

Tumbler

Long an all-time favorite, the overall pattern of this shape can be seen in Photograph 12.

Diagram 102

12. Tumbler. Ca. 1900. 79″ x 101″. This quilt top was discovered in the estate of Dick Swanson's grandparents, and it was quilted in 1983 by Ellen Swanson.

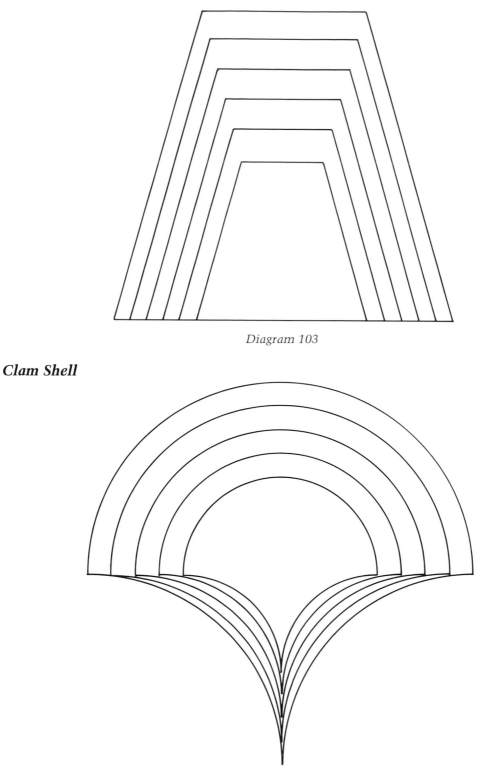

Diagram 103

Clam Shell

Diagram 104

Diagram 105

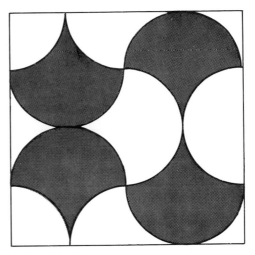

Diagram 106

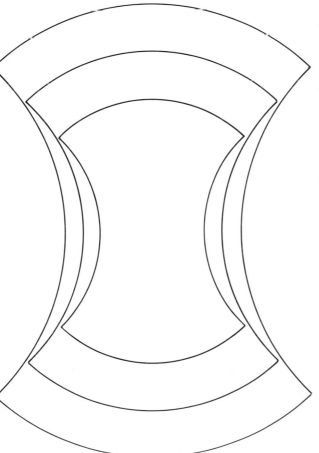

Double Curve

This interesting curved design has several names dating back at least as far as the early 1900s. They are "Friendship Quilt," "Always Friends," "Badge of Friendship," "Charm Quilt," "Mother's Oddity" and "Jigsaw." The names seem to suggest that it may have been a popular design to use for a charm quilt (see Chapter V).

Diagram 107

Diagram 108

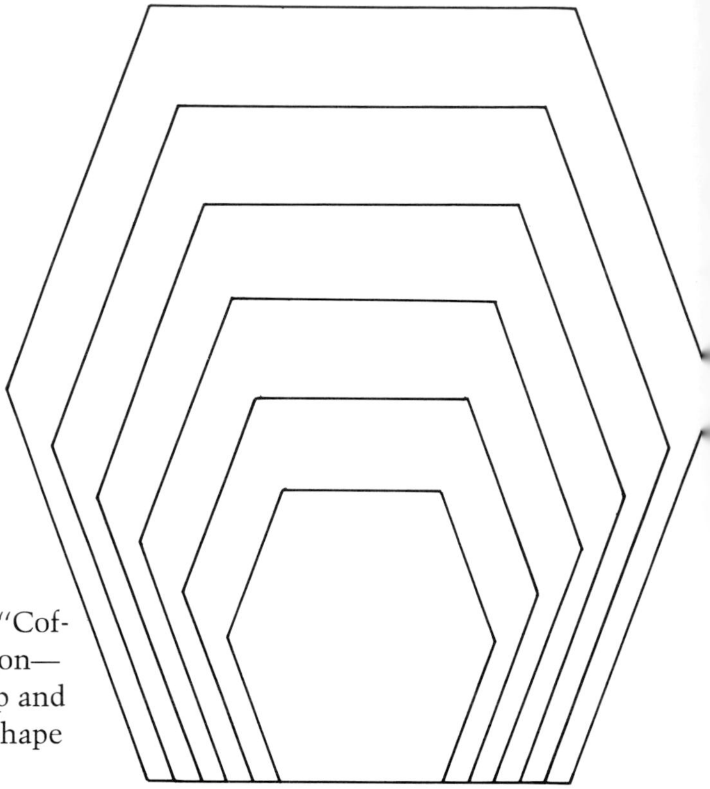

Coffin

The one-patch design known as "Coffin" is actually an elongated hexagon—elongated with a flat side at the top and bottom. A charm quilt using this shape is shown in Photograph 1.

Diagram 109

Honeycomb

The "Honeycomb" is also an elongated hexagon, but this time with the point at the top and bottom.

The second of these two elongated hexagon shapes is the one Emma Tyrell speaks of in Chapter V on charm quilts. The shapes can look very different depending on the severity of the angles and the length of the sides as these two versions demonstrate. These shapes can be colored in any of the same ways that the regular hexagon can. (See the designs in Diagrams 28–32.)

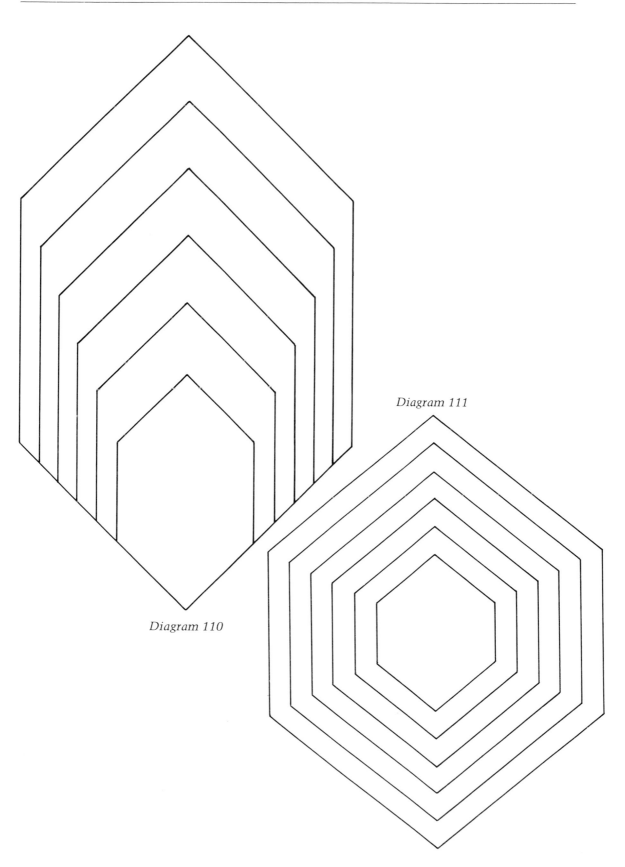

Diagram 111

Diagram 110

Half Honeycomb

The next shape is almost the same as cutting the foregoing Honeycomb in half lengthwise; the only difference is that all three short sides must be exactly the same length. The shape was discovered by Linda Pool on a Suisse franc note (see Photograph 13). She was fascinated with the geometric design on the note and created her quilt, "Francly Radiant" (Color plate 4), from it. Study of the line drawing (Diagram 113) reveals other fascinating ways the design might be colored.

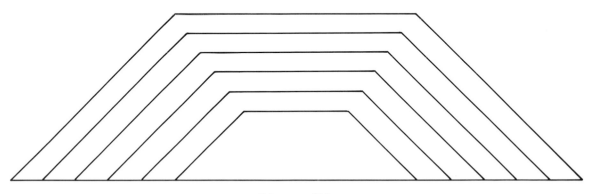

Diagram 112

Diagram 113

13. Suisse Franc note.

Variations on "Nelson's Victory"

The next design forms a cross. It is based on a four-patch and, as a block design, is known as "Nelson's Victory." When the corner squares of the block are eliminated and the crosses intertwine, the design in Diagram 115 occurs. One possible color arrangement is shown next in Diagram 116. The shape can also be put together in an almost braided effect as in the last design (Diagram 117).

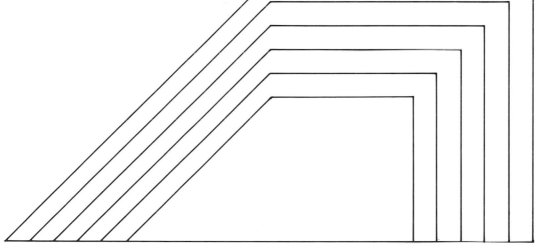

Diagram 114

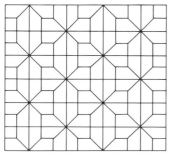

Diagram 115

Diagram 116

Diagram 117

Obtuse Triangle

Judy Spahn used this odd-shaped triangle (Diagram 118) to create the design
for her charm quilt shown in Photograph 14. Note how she has achieved a
folded illusion with her use of contrasts
and proved once again that there are no
limits to the use of imagination in
quiltmaking!

Diagram 118

14. Untitled. Partial charm quilt top pieced by Judy Spahn in 1985.

Repeat Unit Multi-Fabric Quilts

There are no specific "scrapbag quilt patterns." Some designs have become known as scrapbag patterns simply because they have been used more often in this type of quilt. Up to this chapter we have been dealing with scrapbag quilts of overall one-patch designs. In addition to the one-patch there are many other overall quilt designs that can be used very effectively in multi-fabric quilts. Most of these might be called "two-patch" because there are generally two pattern pieces used. The two pieces form a unit which is then repeated throughout the quilt. Some of these units form squares, such as the "Ocean Waves" (see Color plate 12), but in others the units are odd shapes.

TWO-PATCH DESIGNS

The "Flying Geese" pattern is a time-honored favorite of many quiltmakers. This design is particularly effective for a scrap look type of quilt. It is traditionally pieced in rows. I suggest, however, that instead of piecing an entire row, you make partial rows. Then when the time comes to piece them all together, you have more flexibility for moving the units around to get the desired color placement. The design requires a dark/light contrast between the larger and smaller triangles. The larger triangles could be dark with a lighter background or vice versa. The same principles discussed in Chapter II about lights and darks apply to this design. Don't make all of the darks very dark and all of the lights very light. For variety use some medium tones as well. As long as the dark is darker than the light next to it, it will still read as a dark (see Diagram 119). Try to have a good balance in the scale of the prints used. For unity and interest you might try adding a border stripe between the rows.

Several other two-patch designs are shown here. By adhering to the light, medium, dark principles and ideas on texture and color discussed earlier, any of them could make a beautiful scrap quilt.

Diagram 119

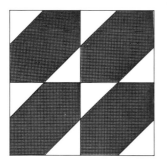

Diagram 120

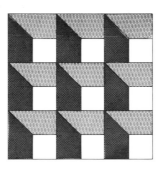

Diagram 121

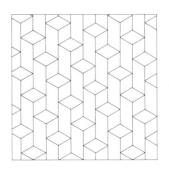

Diagram 122

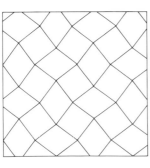

Diagram 123

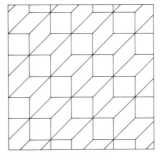

Diagram 124

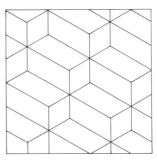

Diagram 125

BLOCK DESIGNS

One-patch and two-patch designs by no means exhaust the supply of patterns that can be used effectively in multi-fabric quilts. Almost any design can be made into a scrap quilt, whether it is a one-patch, block style, medallion or even a scene—as long as care is taken in placement of contrast, texture and color.

Often when choosing fabrics for a quilt using a repeat block for the design, a person will carefully select fabrics for one block and then make all the others the same. Although this makes for a nicely uniform quilt in terms of design and color, it can become boring to construct. Some people find comfort and relaxation in the repetition. For my own temperament, I find that once a block is complete, I don't particularly like to make any others just like it. To me the challenge is in working with many different fabrics within the color scheme and seeing how many versions of the block I can make. I try to make no two identical. Working this way I find that there are some blocks I like better than others, but it is fun to point those out to people when the quilt is complete. Susan Powers, when commenting on her quilt, "Evening Star," (Color plate 7) said, "It was almost anticlimactic to do the quilting. I had such fun playing with the fabrics and making all the blocks different." There is a richness in texture created by using many different fabrics that cannot be achieved with making all of the blocks the same.

Making each block different is not as difficult as one would think. As mentioned earlier in Chapter II, I first plan a quilt in black and white, making several drawings of the design, coloring each in different versions of black, white and medium and then photocopying the drawings. I place the various versions side by side, decide which one I like the best and then use that paste-up as my master plan. That master plan dictates where the dark, medium and light colored fabrics should go in the quilt.

The next decision to make is whether or not all of the dark areas will be the same color or a blending of several dark colors. The same decision needs to be made with the light and medium areas. If you choose to make all the dark areas the same color, but with different fabrics, then you need to sort your fabrics. For "Castle Keep" I chose brown, beige, red, rust, orange and green. There were two alternating versions of the block (see Diagram 1 and 2), but I was consistent with the use of color and darks, mediums and lights in each version. I sorted my fabrics into dark browns, similar tones of red, light beiges, etc. Then I always put dark brown in the same place on the points of the star. I used many different dark brown fabrics, but they appeared in the same place in each block. Every alternate block had light corners. I put beige in those corners, but there were many different beiges. The corners in the other block always had various rust colored fabrics. I always used red in the same position, but many different reds.

Susan Powers used a similar technique in her quilt "Evening Star" (Color plate 7). Susan put more than 40 different fabrics in her quilt and no two blocks are the same. The quilt has a rich texture because of so many fabrics, yet it has unity because she was consistent with her placement of colors. She always used a brown fabric for the points of the star, a beige for the background and a rust for the large spaces. Three fabrics—two paisleys and one border print—were used for the centers of the stars, but she managed to cut those three fabrics in different ways so that all centers are different.

Barbara Bockman likewise was consistent with color placement in her quilt, "Valley Star," (Color plate 10). Even though many different rust and blue fabrics have been incorporated into the quilt the two colors have been used in the same place in each block, giving unity to the design, but because the same rust and blue are not repeated throughout there is an additional texture which lends interest and variety.

You may decide that rather than putting the same color in the dark areas you will use any dark color. For instance if your color scheme is blues and greens, you may always have dark blue and dark green in the dark position. Judy Spahn's quilt, "Stars and Stripes," (Photograph 15), has an overall unity to it that is very appealing; on close examination one realizes that there are many different colors and fabrics in the dark areas. She has used dark green, blue, brown and black prints; but all of them are of a similar intensity and muted so they blend together and give a very pleasing effect. In the light areas she has several different beiges.

In another of Judy's quilts, "Metro" (Color plate 11), she has created an interesting woven effect with the blue fabrics. Her block is actually an octagon which is adjacent to other octagons with yellow squares filling in the empty spaces, as shown in Diagram 126.

Each block is composed of four blue pieces set around a yellow square. Two opposite pieces are dark blue and the other two opposites are light blue. But, again, the darks are not always very dark and the lights not always very light which is what creates the intriguing effect of the lattice turning and winding in and out.

The most important consideration is to adhere to your black and white mockup of the design concerning the placement of dark, medium and light fabrics. If sometimes you use light fabrics in a certain place and at other times dark or medium, you may get a hodgepodge effect.

Another device that can give unity to a block style quilt of many different fabrics is to repeat one fabric in the same part of the design throughout. This could be using the same background fabric, for example, or a border print in the same place in each block. The unifying fabrics in "Castle Keep" were the border prints. I used two different border prints, each in the alternate blocks, between the points of the star. The unifying factor in Judy Spahn's "Stars and Stripes" is the grey and black striped fabric in each block.

The beautiful eight-pointed star quilt (shown in Color plate 1) has many different fabrics in the stars, but they are

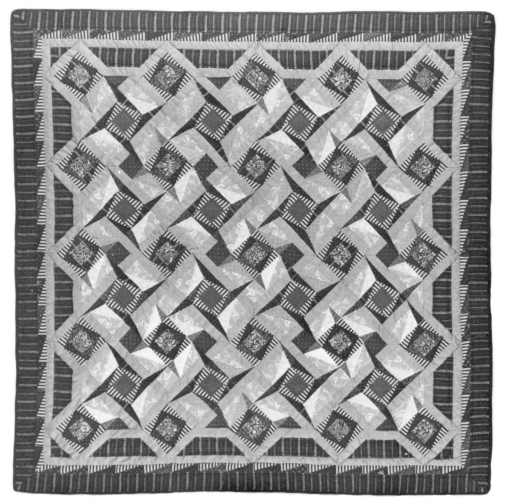

15. Stars and Stripes. 54″ x 54″. Made by Judy Spahn in 1984. Predominant colors are rust, grey and black.

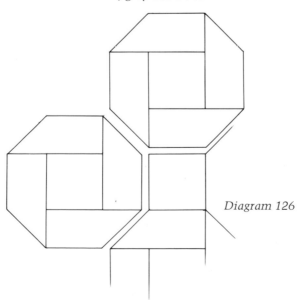

Diagram 126

16. Eight-pointed Star. Detail of Color plate 1.

of similar subtle colors. The unifying factor in that quilt is the broderie perse appliquéd flowers between the stars. (See the black and white close-up, Photograph 16.)

The "Album Patch" quilt (Photograph 17) has many different fabrics in the squares, but unity is provided by the consistent use of light centers in the blocks as well as the dark squares

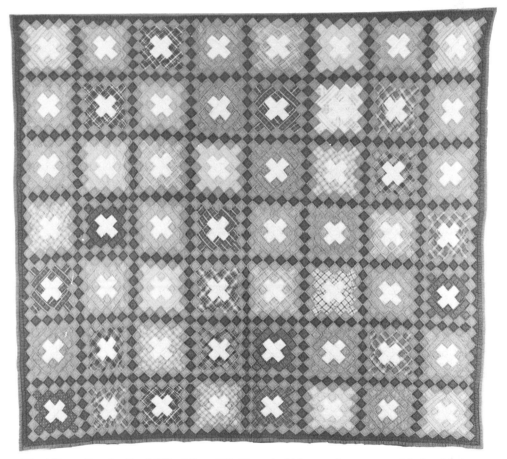

17. Album Patch. Ca. 1900. 66″ × 73″. Pieced of blue, red, orange and beige fabrics.
From the collection of Linda Pool.

around the blocks.

One needs to be careful when making a block style quilt if the traditional interpretation of the design calls for only two or three fabrics. It is difficult to use a lot of different colors in such a quilt without getting a spotty effect. For instance if you have a ten-inch block there will be a high concentration of a single color, and if many of the blocks are of different colors the brighter ones will jump out. For larger sized blocks it might be best to stick to multiple fabrics of the same or similar colors, or to alternate blocks every other one with two different colors.

The quilt top shown in Photographs 18 and 19 has a fairly large block with only two fabrics in each block. In each case muslin has been combined with either a dark brown or a dark blue fabric; but because the fabrics, whether blue or brown, are all very dark and of a smiliar tone, they blend well together.

With smaller blocks of six or seven inches, some of the stronger colors can be used in several of the blocks and then balanced throughout the quilt.

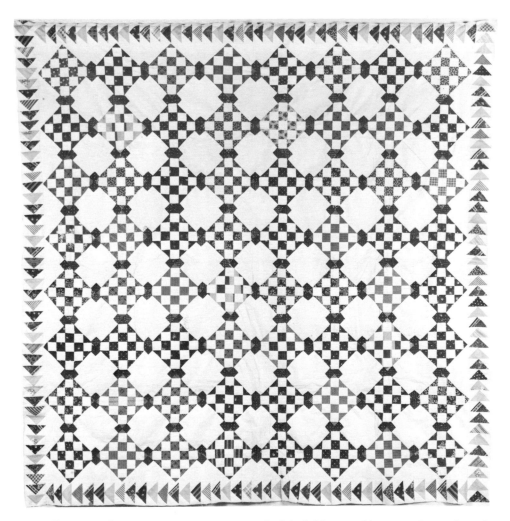

18. Album Patch Variation. 78″ x 80″. Pieced of dark blues and browns. From the collection of Diana Leone.

19. Album Patch Variation. Detail.

Designs which contain narrow strips such as the "Pineapple" (Photograph 20) or "Log Cabin" work exceedingly well in the scrap look. Here again it is important to have shadings of the various colors. Both of these designs have light and dark parts in each block. But the dark parts don't have to be very dark as long as overall they read darker than the light parts. Look at the close-

20. Pineapple. Ca. 1890. 80" x 80". Made in Leesburg, Virginia. From the collection of Dick and Ellen Swanson.

21. Pineapple. Detail.

up of the "Pineapple" quilt (Photograph 21). There are several intensities of darks and lights which make it much more interesting than if all of the darks had been very dark and all of the lights very light. Notice also the richness of texture that has been achieved through the variety of fabrics that have been used.

See the difference in the "Log Cabin"

blocks in Diagrams 127 and 128. Diagram 128 with several shadings of the lights and darks is more pleasing than Diagram 127 in which all of the darks are very dark and the lights very light.

With the "Log Cabin" and "Pine-apple" designs, just as with other repeat unit patterns, it is not only more fun to do each block a little differently, but the end results are visually more rewarding.

Diagram 127

Diagram 128

Charm Quilts

A type of quilt long neglected in the reporting of the history of quilt-making in the United States is the charm quilt. It is a style of quilt so prevalent, yet perhaps so ordinary looking to the casual observer that it was easy to pass over as just another scrap quilt. It has only been in recent years that we have become newly aware of this type of quilt, and can appreciate the thought and process involved in making it.

A charm quilt is a quilt—usually a one-patch—in which no two patches are cut from the same fabric. Charm quilts were most popular between 1860 and 1900, but had a comeback interest in the 1920s and 30s. Many of the quilts were random patches of the different fabrics, as in the two charm quilts shown in Photographs 1 and 22. In most of those I have seen, however, there was a definite attempt to create some type of overall design whether it was a simple light/dark placement of pieces as in the quilt shown in Photograph 24 or a more elaborate overall design such as those shown in Photo-

graph 26 and Color plates 15, 16, 17, 20.

One reason charm quilts may have gone unnoticed for so many years is that they look like most other scrap quilts. So many of the fabrics of the late 1800s were very similar to each other and without close scrutiny it's hard to tell them apart. For instance there must have been hundreds of varieties of those pink fabrics that were so popular during the 1870s, which many of us now refer to as the "bubble gum pinks." The "Thousand Pyramids" charm quilt (Color plate 18) and the hexagon (Color plate 20) both use those pink fabrics. I counted 31 different ones in the hexagon quilt and almost 100 in the "Thousand Pyramids." I could not find any of the pinks duplicated in the two quilts, so that makes at least 131 different ones in the 1870s when those two quilts were probably made. Of course some of the fabrics may have been found in fabric scraps saved by mothers or grandmothers, but still the variety is impressive.

We tend to think that because it was a hundred years ago that there were not

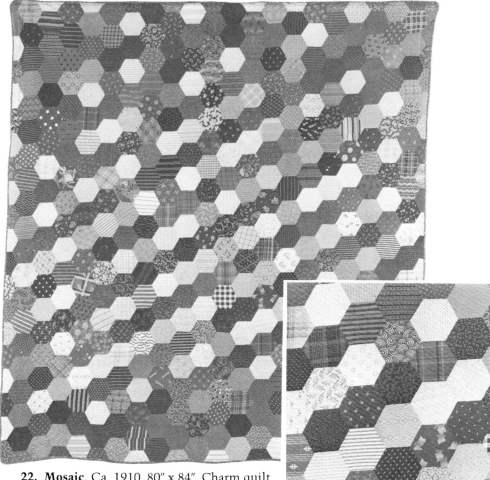

22. Mosaic. Ca. 1910. 80″ x 84″. Charm quilt
with 420 different pieces. From the collection
of Diana Leone.

23. Mosaic. Detail.

a variety of fabrics available and that it
would be impossible to find enough different ones for a quilt. There are stories
of it taking several years to collect
enough fabric for a charm quilt. Some
collecting even carried into another
generation. But fabrics were available.
There were probably as many different

fabrics being printed in the fourth
quarter of the 19th century as there are
now. We forget that to be fashionable
was as important to women then as it
is now. Fabric styles and prints contin-
ually changed. In an article in 1852,
Godey's Ladys Book stated:
"The spring or the winter fashions of

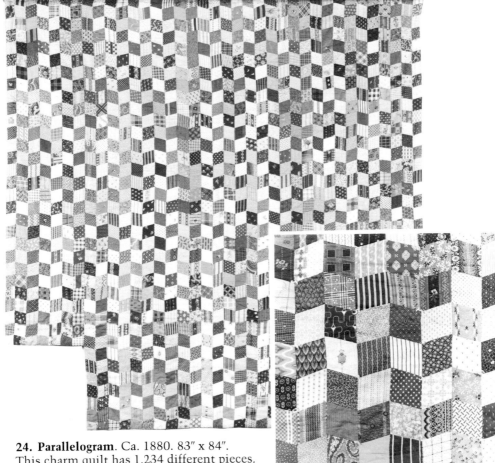

24. Parallelogram. Ca. 1880. 83″ x 84″. This charm quilt has 1,234 different pieces, including a centennial fabric with the dates 1776–1876. Author's collection.

25. Parallelogram. Detail. Just as with the quilt in Color plates 20 and 21, care has been taken to make all of the striped fabrics in the quilt go in the same direction.

each year must be <u>new</u>; and although millions of patterns have preceded those of any particular year, yet the patterns each year must be stamped with the characteristic of novelty, or they will not sell . . . it is the business of a peculiar set of artists or pattern designers to furnish the printer with a large variety of designs, from which he selects those which he thinks likely to suit the taste of his customers."[1]

Cuesta Benberry, in her article on charm quilts in the March 1980 issue of *Quilter's Newsletter*, probably became the first person to rekindle the interest in charm quilts in this decade. That

26. Triangles. Ca. 1880. 72″ x 72″. Charm quilt from Michigan made of 480 different pieces. Note the white star in the center. From the collection of Dick and Ellen Swanson.

27. Triangles. Detail.

article not only made us aware of the existence of this type of quilt, but made us want to try one ourselves. It also put us on the lookout for old charm quilts. That search has brought me to the realization that charm quilts were as prevalent—or more so—during the late 1800s as crazy quilts. We have just been more aware of crazy quilts because their style, unique fabrics and stitchery make them much more visible.

There is very little published about charm quilts. Anything written on sewing or related projects during the late 1800s was about fancy work, patchwork with silk and velvet, lacemaking and so on. Cotton was considered ordinary and unworthy of mention in the women's books of the times. All literature seemed to echo the sentiments of Mrs. Pullan who in 1859 said:

"Of the patchwork with calico, I have

nothing to say. Valueless indeed must be the time of that person who can find no better use for it than to make ugly counterpanes and quilts of pieces of cotton."[2]

Patchwork with cotton was considered more a way for young girls to learn to sew or for older women who no longer had the eyesight for fancier work. Nevertheless, the fact remains that there were thousands of quilts made of cotton during that time, and many of those were charm quilts. My guess is that most of them were made by young girls—perhaps their first endeavors at quilting. The workmanship on the samples I have seen is not as intricate as that of other quilts of the period.

The fact that so many charm quilts made in the late 1800s exist is evidence enough that there was a fad or trend toward making them. All we can do is combine the small bits and pieces of information that are available and form our own conclusions.

The first question that comes to mind is how did charm quilts get their name? Some authorities suggest, as Cuesta Benberry does in her article, that "the allure of the huge variety of material scraps needed to make them accounts for the name—charm quilts."[3] Emma S. Tyrrell wrote in *Wallace's Farmer* in 1929: "Our grandmothers endeavored to make these quilts with no two pieces alike—that is where the charm lies—in the many different fascinating colors used."[4]

I believe the name goes back as well to another definition of charm: something to bring good luck. Webster's dic-tionary defines charm not only as "a trait that fascinates, allures, or delights" but also as "the chanting or reciting of a magic spell, an act or expression believed to have magic power, something worn about the person to ward off evil or ensure good fortune." The little bit of information I have been able to gather on charm quilts of the 1800s suggests that the use of so many different fabrics offered allure and the quilts themselves wove some kind of magic or brought good luck.

During the same time that charm quilts were becoming such a rage (around 1860) there were other equally as popular "charm collections." There were "charm bottles", for example, that were covered with beeswax in which were embedded buttons, mementos and small charms.

"Charm strings," another Victorian fad from around 1860 to 1900, were made by collecting different buttons and putting them on strings. More is written about the button collections than any of the other charm fads. The *National Button Bulletin* for September, 1948 had an article on charm strings which gives insight into the collections:

"These charm strings were made primarily of buttons but the young ladies generally strung upon them a few amulets, steeped in sentiment. Some tokens were from the boys who made their hearts beat faster, others were precious because of childhood or schooldays association. Among the most popular charms were dimes, gold dollars, tiny baskets whittled from pecan, hazlenut

28. Charm String. Ca. 1875. Photograph courtesy of the State Museum of Pennsylvania, Pennsylvania Historical and Museum Commission.

and almond shells, or peach pits, little seashells, tiny doll arms and legs, miniature merrythoughts, dolls, jugs, keys, horseshoes and religious medals.

While Johnie was satisfied with a rabbit's foot in his pocket to protect himself from harm, Sister Mary fortified herself with every charm available. But for her, the charm string was not so much a guard to repel harm. Rather it was a chain of sentimental symbols, dear to her heart, which she cherished in the faith that it would attract good fortune."[5]

There are various stories connected with the charm strings. The most prevalent is that when a girl had collected 999 different buttons on the string her true love would come along with the 1,000th on his coat, and the couple would live happily ever after. Elinor Graham wrote a book in 1947 called *The Maine Charm String,* after she had moved to Maine and become interested in collecting buttons. She came across several charm strings in her search and wrote about the 999 button superstition. "The charm didn't always work," she writes. "Of the four charm strings that I have received as a gift, or have bought, three were the work of maiden ladies."[6]

Jane Adams, co-editor of the *National Button Bulletin,* has told me that it was believed that if a girl made the mistake of putting 1,000 buttons on her string she would end up being an old maid. Perhaps those three charm strings that Elinor Graham wrote about bore the curse of containing 1,000 buttons!

On the other hand, not all women felt they needed 999 buttons. Among the grandmother collectors the *National Button Bulletin* writes about was one who expressed a sentiment which seemed to prevail generally among them: "Land sakes! When George came along, I didn't need the 999th button!"[7]

Another story about the charm strings is that a girl believed that when the string was as long as she was tall, she would be married.

Elinor Graham related some of her own feelings about charm strings in her book:

"When Mrs. McKee poured out the buttons on her kitchen table she said: 'Art's mother and a friend collected these. It was kind of a fad when they was girls. You could have looked at them better when they was on the string . . . They were called charm strings,' she said. 'They tried to get nine hundred and ninety-nine—all different, no two alike. I can't remember rightly now, but the buttons was to work some kind of charm.'. . . I ran through the buttons once very quickly; then again more slowly. There is no explaining the fascination of an old charm string. Unless you are moved by the thought of a young girl stringing fashion and history, color and design on one cord, with love as the motivating force, you will not be interested in a complete description of a charm string."[8]

Young girls devised various methods of collecting buttons for their strings. Their first buttons probably came from the button boxes of their mothers and grandmothers. Once they exhausted those supplies they would trade with friends or play certain games. One of the buttons on the string was called the "touch button." Some books say it was the first button put on the string, others say it was the most conspicuous one. If friends were together admiring each others' strings, when one touched the "touch button," the owner of the button could select the handsomest button from her friend's string.[9] If a young gentleman came to call and the charm string was brought out for him to admire if he touched the "touch button" "he would be startled by a sharp exclamation of seeming surprise from the young hostess, 'Oh dear! You have touched the charm button! Now you will have to give me a button for my string.' "[10]

"It was quite usual for young men to purchase buttons at the dry goods to bestow upon these fair collectors. Certainly there was no gesture in that day which would ingratiate them more, or establish their reputations as charming gentlemen. When women and girls had dresses made and got buttons to trim them, they bought a few extra ones to give to their charm string friends. In many instances these collectors practiced patience while a gown served its usefulness, but felt rewarded when finally its buttons were shared among them."[11]

It was considered bad luck to purchase buttons for their own string; the buttons on the string that were gifts supposedly indicated how many friends a person had. So there would be no doubt about where her buttons came from, Mary Ann Fritz chose to mount her buttons on a board instead of a string. Under each button she wrote the name of the donor (Photograph 30). Girls would enjoy talking about their buttons and might have exaggerated

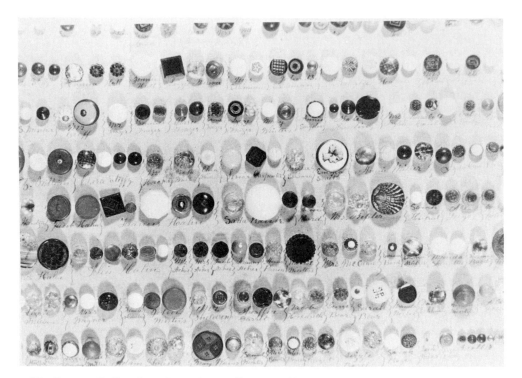

29. Button Collection. Ca. 1872. Collection of buttons assembled and mounted by Mary Ann Fritz. The buttons are still on the original sheet with names of each of the persons from whom they were obtained. All the buttons are from civilian dresses and coats of the period and most are ladies' buttons. Photograph courtesy of the State Museum of Pennsylvania, Pennsylvania Historical and Museum Commission.

their worth or importance. " 'Aunt Lillie gave me this one from a dress she wore attending the Inaugural Ball in Washington.' 'Old Mrs. Gray told me that this one came off her grandfather's uniform.' 'May Whitney traded me this one for that old calico one you gave me.' "[12]

The idea of collecting different fabric samples from friends and relatives as mementos to be sewn into a quilt follows right in line with the collecting of buttons. The little information I have gleaned about charm quilts indicates that the fabrics for those quilts were also collected by young girls. Ellen Swanson, while antique hunting, found several stacks of triangles sewn together to form a square. All of the fabrics (dating from the 1870s) were different. Sewn to the top of each stack was a little note. They said, "Mama's dresses and waists—six sewed," "My eldest sister Jessie's dresses—3 sewed," "32 sewed—most all of Aunt Ellen's." (See Photograph 30.) The writer, probably a young girl, appears to have been collecting the pieces for her charm quilt, keeping track of them in this manner until she had enough for her quilt.

Bertha M. Weiler who lives in Baldwin, Kansas, has a charm quilt in a "Tumbling Blocks" pattern which her mother made in the 1880s. Each piece in the quilt is different and Bertha says that when her mother was a teenager she traded fabrics with her friends to get enough for her quilt.[13] And still another account of a charm quilt made by a young girl appears in a catalog of a quilt exhibit held at the Mitchell Museum in Mt. Vernon, Illinois, March–April 1979, called *In Praise of Patchwork*:

"This quilt was especially made for the trousseau of the quilter and contains no two fabrics that are alike. In those days ladies of the communities often traded fabric and when Miss Lemon discovered a repetition she quickly removed the duplicate and added another. Tragically she died before marrying and this quilt is treasured by her niece."[14]

Charm quilts have also been known as friendship or memory quilts. An exhibit of quilts in Toronto called "Pieced Quilts of Ontario" had two charm quilts. One was actually called a charm quilt and was made about 1880. It had 780 elongated hexagons—each one different and supposedly from a different person bringing good luck to the user. Another quilt of the "Tumbling Blocks" pattern was described in the catalog: "The donor called this a 'friendship' quilt because each piece had been given

30. Charm Quilt Patches. Ca. 1880. From the collection of Dick and Ellen Swanson.

to the maker, her mother Sarah Doane (Lundy) Daly, by a different friend. The quilt was made about 1870 in the Newmarket area of York Country."[15]

From the information I can find, I believe that the charm quilts of the late 1800s were made by young girls out of superstition, as good luck charms or for memorics of their many friends. While a young button collector's heart might skip a beat when she looked at the button she had collected off her heart-throb's coat, a young charm quiltmaker might be equally excited by fabric that matched her boyfriend's shirt. The girls probably collected fabric from friends and relatives, vying with one another to see how many different ones they could stitch into a quilt. They perhaps even devised their own version of the "touch button" game, based on the way the fabrics were put together. Two of the quilts I have seen have one fabric which has been used twice. I wonder if it was put in deliberately to make someone find the repeated fabric, or if it was just a mistake? Working with so many pieces makes it hard to remember what you have already used.

The maker of the "Thousand Pyramids" quilt (Color plate 18) made a definite attempt to put almost identical fabrics side by side. (See close up view 19.) You could swear they were identical until you looked closely and discovered that the colors, the stripes, the prints or whatever varied ever so slightly.

The hexagon quilt in Color plate 20 has used many striped fabrics. All of those stripes are going in the same direction. (See close-up 21.)

Despite the number of stories about the quilts with 999 pieces, I have heard of only one such quilt. Likewise, very few button strings with 999 buttons have been found. The one quilt I know of was brought to my attention by Mona Clark of New Hampshire. Her friend, Paula Scruton, told of a Tumbler quilt made in 1910 and owned by her cousin's family. It has exactly 999 pieces—27 across and 37 down. Another quilt comes close: the one shown in Color plate 15 has exactly 997 pieces.

More important than the superstition attached to the number of pieces, no doubt, were the memories evoked by the fabrics, the buttons or other mementos. Consider this report I found in a book called *The Charm String* written in 1943:

"Last summer a boy I know spent six weeks in the country visiting his grandmother and grandfather. When he came home in time to go to school, he brought with him a little box. He seemed to think the box was very important. In it, among other odds and ends of things, were a fishhook, a small red stone, a buckle, and a button. I asked him why these things were valuable to him.

Proudly he told me that the fishhook was what he had caught his first fish with—a good-sized trout, which he had eaten for breakfast the next morning. The stone came from a hill on the farm where he had had many picnics. The buckle was from the harness of the pony he had been allowed to ride during the summer. The button had been given him by an Army airplane pilot who had visited the farm on furlough. It had been on the uniform the pilot was wearing when he had shot down an enemy plane over the Pacific Ocean.

As the boy told me about the objects in the box, I saw why they were valuable to him. Each thing stood for something that he liked to remember. People have always collected such mementos. Years ago, many children collected mementos which could be strung on a string. . . . The charm string which this book tells about was just such a collection of mementos."[15]

Young boys and girls have always enjoyed collecting things, whether it be buttons, fabric, baseball cards, stamps, coins, stickers, rocks or beer cans. Part of the enjoyment is trading with friends, ooing and awing over what someone else has, fingering the items, remembering where the different ones came from. It surely must have been the same with collecting the many fabrics for a charm quilt.

There was a renewed interest in charm quilts as well as other "collections" of mementos during the 1920s and 30s. My daughter has inherited my mother's charm bracelet from that period. When I asked my mother about the significance of the bracelet, she said collecting the charms for it was just a fad. Yet each charm brings back memories to her.

Linda Horton from Somers, New York, has a charm quilt made by her grandmother, Bernice White Horton, who is now 89. The quilt was probably made in the 1920s or early 30s. I asked her to find out any information she could about the quilt and she wrote

back: "My grandmother did not remember anything about 'charm' quilts, per se, but did remember that women liked to make quilts that were all different and would buy scrap bags to do so."

From Rochester, New Hampshire, Mona Clark wrote to me about charm quilts of New England:

"I wonder if different sections of the country each have their own traditions about said quilts? I would like to share a New Hampshire version with you— the Charm quilts made here during the depression years contained 999 pieces, and each piece was of a different fabric. A friend from here, Pauline Scruton, told me it took her years to collect enough fabrics from friends and family members for her charm quilt. The traditional pattern was the Tumbler design.

The story that goes with my friend's quilt is that whenever you sleep under a charm quilt for the first time, whatever you dream will come true. Years ago she visited her cousin and slept under her newly finished charm quilt and proceeded to have one of the worst dreams of her life (she still remembers it and described it to me). She awoke with a start, but to her great relief, the quilt had slipped to the floor during the night. She chose to believe that this had happened BEFORE her dream, so she felt quite relieved, needless to say."

By the 1920s and 30s charm quilts were no longer fads of young girls. It was the granddaughters of those who had made them earlier who now wanted to try their hand at charm quilts because they had heard their grandmothers talk about them. By this time, however, the fabrics, colors and prints had changed so drastically that it was no longer esthetically pleasing to put so many fabrics side by side in a quilt. The charm quilts that evolved still used all different fabrics, but now a plain block might be alternated with a patterned block, or sashing strips may have separated the blocks. We see many quilts from this time in the "Sun Bonnet Sue" pattern (each "Sun Bonnet Sue" is of a different fabric) or "Grandmother's Flower Garden" in which each flower is different. The first published material about charm quilts appeared in this era. It was usually printed in a newspaper quilting or needlework column as a pattern or an account of a quilt that had been made two generations earlier. There were even advertisements offering packets of all different fabrics such as the following which appeared in an early 1930s issue of the *California Cultivator*: "Those of you who have exhausted your scrapbook of desirable prints will find this package a regular 'gold mine' of lovely small figured prints. Everyone is different and of course color-fast. There are 25 different pieces about 4 x 9 in size and a 15¢ cutting pattern free with each package." In the January 18, 1929, issue of *Wallace's Farmer*, Emma Tyrrell gave a pattern for a charm quilt which was an elongated hexagon. She wrote:

"*The entire quilt is pieced of these six-sided blocks. Our grandmothers endeavored to make these quilts with no two pieces alike . . . they exchanged scraps of fabrics with friends to get variety. Many succeeded, as two of the quilts I have seen testify. One was*

made of a much smaller design than this one. I would like a quilt made from this design with the center of each block white; that would give uniform patches of white over the quilt and form a pretty contrast to the figured fabrics."[17]

A wonderful article appeared in the April 13, 1971, issue of *Cappers Weekly* in which Mildred Smith describes charm quilts begun by her mother and her aunt when they were girls during the late 1800s:

SIX GENERATIONS PIECED INTO CHARM QUILT

"*I have been renewing my family history memories—not with pen and paper but with needle and thread.*

Years ago my mother and her sister each started making a Charm Quilt. What the 'charm' was I've never known, but it was made of small hexagons, each of different material, no two alike. Grandmother's scrap bag was the principal source, but with 2,400 to 2,500 hexagons required, various relatives contributed and scraps were exchanged with neighbors. Such a long time was required to accumulate so many different blocks that the partially-pieced quilt tops were put away during school and teaching years and busy early-married days. Years later, after I was grown, both quilts were completed and eventually one went to my young grandson for his single bed.

Now in need of replacements for a few worn blocks, the quilt was handed to Grandmother (me this time) for repair. What memories the pieces evoked!

The one of the greatest interest is the green with indistinct brown plaid, a piece of the last dress yardage bought by my great-grandfather for my grandmother before her marriage. Let's see—she was married in Virginia in 1871! Why, that piece is 100 years old! Doubtless bought from a peddler's wagon. I wonder—did she take the material with her and make the dress after she was a bride, in Kentucky? And carry the scraps in their later moves to Nebraska, then to western Kansas? Thank goodness, that piece shows no sign of wear.

Other old pieces—gingham, chambray, and calico—bring back childhood memories, some of garments worn by Grandmother and aunties, and many more familiar as pieces from the "scrap bag." Dots, stripes, checks, and quaint old figures. Horseshoes seemed to be popular figures—probably shirts worn by my uncles as they herded cattle on the buffalo grass prairie and attended country school.

This little red-and-white print—the very first of my own dresses that I can remember! And this piece was my sister's, and another from a pinafore made me by Auntie. And Mother's housedresses and aprons—I can almost smell the homemade bread and cinnamon rolls, the spicy pickling vinegar, and the grape jelly from her kitchen! This piece is from a dress she wore before my little brother was born. Here's the yellow with broken black stripe that was rag doll Fern's dress. And my teddy bear's shirt!

Around the sides, as the quilt was added to in later years, are scraps from the next generation, dresses my sisters and I wore. The auburn-haired sister had the blues, browns and greens; mousey me the reds and pinks. My desire was always lavender, but no, "lavender is for old ladies." So here is the little lavender-and-white check, the material I bought to make my first dress in Domestic Art (Home Ec, to you.)

For the replacement hexagons I'm appliqueing on, I am using bits from our daughters' dresses and one from Son's shirt, and from the few dresses I've made for granddaughters. Just to make the 100 year cycle and 6-generation record complete, I'll use this maroon-and-tan broadcloth from Grandson's pajamas.

Proud as he is of the old quilt Grandmother gave him, it was at his request that the renovation was undertaken, I'm not sure that such an historic item shouldn't be preserved instead of used. But, on the other hand, after I'm gone, what will these bits of memory mean to anyone else? Let him enjoy using it."[18]

The newly revived interest in charm quilts suggests that perhaps the revivals go in more or less 50 year cycles. First the 1870s and 80s, then the 1920s and 30s and now the 1980s. I became interested in charm quilts through my friend Ellen Swanson from Fairfax, Virginia, who is probably the person most responsible for the current interest in Northern Virginia. In fact I think I can say without a doubt that there are more charm quilts being made at this time in

Northern Virginia than in any other part of the United States.

Ellen attended a quilt show organized by Pat Long from Baltimore. In that show Pat exhibited several pieces of her students' work, among which were some charm quilts. Ellen became very excited about making a charm quilt herself and soon organized a group with several of her quilting friends, each of whom was to make a charm quilt. Several of the members of the group are now on their second charm quilt, and Kathryn Kuhn is quilting her fourth. Two of Kathryn's charm quilts are shown in this book (Photographs 3 and 5). There were no specific rules set up concerning the charm quilts made in the group except an underlying assumption that no one was allowed to purchase fabric. It must either come from the quilter's own collections or from a friend's. I might have been better off if I had joined that group. My charm quilt ended up being the most expensive quilt I ever made. Even though I had a lot of fabric and was given much more by students and friends, to complete the quilt in my chosen color scheme, I needed even more and could not resist walking into every fabric shop I saw. No shop would sell less than an eighth of a yard. I made no attempt to keep track of how many eighth yard pieces I purchased. I don't think I want to know. The good part of it is that I have many pretty pieces that I can now share with friends for their charm quilts.

A charm quilt brings out many special feelings. I doubt that, today, they have anything to do with the earlier superstitious or sentimental hopes of young girls. In fact, all of the women I know who are making charm quilts are already married. Some of the special feelings surely stem from the memories these quilts stir up. A large part of the feelings have to do with the fabrics themselves—with the joy of collecting and handling so many of them. And much of the joy of making a charm quilt comes from the relative freedom it allows you to do your own thing. With so many different fabrics to handle, you can't be expected to do wonderful things; so you experiment, play with the fabrics and in the end create something that you never thought possible!

I called several of my friends who have made charm quilts and out of the blue asked them how they felt about making them. I didn't pose the question and ask them to think about it. I just wanted their immediate reaction. The response was universal. Everyone said making charm quilts was fun.

Kathryn Kuhn from Annandale, Virginia, said, "I like making them because it's the most fun I've ever had. The most fun part of any quilt is playing with the fabrics. Once that is done it's downhill from there on. The nice thing about a charm quilt is that you keep doing the best part."

Yoko Sawanoboro from Rockville, Maryland, talked about her experience with her charm quilt. She reminded me of a meeting we had had at my house and how Barbara Bockman had come with a box of fabric scraps. Barbara said that she had just cleaned her workroom and was trying to get rid of some things. She wanted everyone to take pieces from the box because she wasn't going to take any of it home with her. Yoko had heard about charm quilts and had been intrigued, but never had had enough different fabrics of her own to start one. She was easily caught up in the enthusiasm of cutting pieces from Barbara's box. She said, "After I came home, I started cutting triangles for my charm quilt and I got the fever. I had so much fun!

Jay Romano from Fairfax, Virginia, said, "I loved it. It was fun! It is something that once you start you can't leave alone. Like eating peanuts. It becomes obsessive." Jay was a part of Ellen Swanson's original group. She said, "The most fun was sharing fabrics. We would meet at a different person's house each week and go through her fabrics." (Jay's quilt is shown in Color plate 5.)

Kay Lettau feels that friendships are created and nurtured through making a charm quilt. Talking of the group that meets to make charm quilts, she said, "We meet with a common bond. We are of different ages and come from different backgrounds, but the needle brings us together and creates friends. There is less pressure in making a charm quilt. I didn't have any expectations. My quilt began as something to do with my friends. So many of the pieces came from friends. When I got a fabric from one of them I figured a way to use it. My quilt is full of uglys and lots of quaint and it turned out much better than any expectations I ever had for it."

"I enjoyed making my charm quilt more than anything I have ever done," said Lenore Parham from Vienna, Virginia, "because I like fabrics and have collected small pieces of many of them. Making a charm quilt allowed me to be able to use all of my fabrics, but not use any of them up. It was just fun playing with them. It is also wonderful to have little things ready to take with you. [Lenore is the only person I know who has 999 different fabrics in her quilt (see Color plate 9).] Having to work within certain limits makes you stretch your imagination," she added, "I love the idea of 999."

Fay Goldey wanted to make a charm quilt of all red prints. She calls her quilt "Big Red" (Color plate 6). She wrote to friends all over the country and asked them to send her a piece of red fabric. She said it became exciting to go to the mail box every day. She vowed she would use them all in her quilt. When I asked her how she felt about making that quilt, she replied, "It was the most fun I ever had. You could kind of go free—with absolute abandon. You don't have to stay within anyone else's guidelines. I laughed when I saw some of the prints people sent me and wondered how I could ever use them. But I did. You can just have fun with this kind of quilt."

Ellen Swanson from Fairfax, Virginia, said, "I'll tell you. To someone like me who has had a long time love affair with fabric (even before I started quilting I was collecting it) a charm quilt has a special attraction. It's so exciting to use some of each piece in a project. The quilt is full of memories and it's a challenge to try to get something reasonably good looking out of a myriad of fabrics. It's just plain fun! And when I leave all these fabrics behind, it's going to be redeeming that I've cut at least a little bit from each one.

I hope you will find making a charm quilt as exciting as the young women of the late 1800s did or as much fun as the women of today. Pick your shape—perhaps one of the patterns given in this book will appeal to you—and start cutting.

P.S.

I have two sons and a daughter. My daughter Kiran is now 14 and is the youngest. From the time she can remember I have been quilting. Whenever the two of us are in the company of other quilters, there is the common question put to her, "Do you quilt?" Or when people ask me about my children, they never fail to ask if my daughter quilts. My answer and hers has always been that she likes quilts and appreciates what I do, but hasn't been interested in doing one herself. I've always known she could make a quilt if she wanted because she is very good with her hands.

My mother always did beautiful flower arranging and worked wonders in the garden. To this day I feel totally incapable of artistically arranging flowers and I feel inept in the garden. I think when a mother does something that she is known for, the child is apt to feel intimidated. Knowing this and understanding how I felt as a child, I never pushed Kiran into sewing. I always felt that if she wanted to do it she would ask. From time to time as she was growing up she would say she wanted to sew a pillow or some other small project, and I would help her to decide upon a pattern and cut a few pieces. Her project would last one or two days at most, and then she would lose interest. I always felt that the pressure of having your work compared to something your mother does might be a very difficult thing to deal with so I encouraged her in any other areas in which she became interested, and knew as she got older when the time came that she decided to make a quilt, if ever, that she would be very capable of doing her own thing.

Kiran watched me making my charm quilt and helped me with the placement of some of the pieces. I always ask various members of my family to give me their reactions to something I am working on, and she contributes her share of advice. After I wrote the rough draft of this chapter on charm quilts she found it lying on the table and picked it up and read through it. Within an hour she came to me and said, "I want to make a charm quilt. I have those pieces that Hanne de Konig from Holland gave me when she visited us. I can use those and remember her in my quilt." Kiran also remembered some fabrics with Teddy bears on them that she bought last year because she thought they were so cute. "I know you wouldn't use them in a quilt, but I like them and they will make me remember the time I bought them when I worked at the Quilting Congress. In fact I want to find a lot of fabrics with animals or objects on them. I just want to use a square or triangle—nothing complicated. This type of quilt doesn't need to be complicated when you are just saving memories."

Her enthusiasm was exciting to see. She was making a quilt in which it was all right to be humble, if she wanted to be, one in which there would be no pressure and from which she could derive a lot of pleasure. I helped her make a template for her pattern, showed her how she should cut the pieces according to the grain line on the fabric and set her loose among my supply of fabrics to cut from those pieces that appealed to her.

"Maybe I can get 999 different fabrics," she said with a gleam in her eye. I wondered if any of her friends would soon be collecting and trading fabrics for their charm quilts . . . waiting for the day when prince charming would come riding up . . .

FOOTNOTES

1. *Godey's Lady's Book*, August 1852, p. 121.
2. Pullan, Mrs., *The Lady's Manual of Fancy-Work*, p. 95.
3. *Quilter's Newsletter Magazine*, March 1980, p. 14.
4. *Wallaces' Farmer*, January 1929, p. 91.
5. *The National Button Bulletin*, September 1948, p. 334.
6. Graham, Elinor, *The Maine Charm String*.
7. *The National Button Bulletin*, p. 334.
8. Graham, Elinor, *The Maine Charm String*.
9. Palenske, Bess Torian, *The Charm String*, p. 12.
10. *The National Button Bulletin*, p. 334.
11. *The National Button Bulletin*, p. 334.
12. Roberts, Catherine, *Who's Got the Button?*, p. 27.
13. *Influences*, p.15.
14. *In Praise of Patchwork*, p. 41.
15. Burnham, Dorothy K., *Pieced Quilts of Ontario*, p. 20.
16. Palenske, p. vii.
17. *Wallaces' Farmer*, p. 91.
18. *Capper's Weekly*, April 13, 1971.

BIBLIOGRAPHY

Bacon, Albion Fellows. *The Charm String*. Indiana: LC Page & Company, 1929.

Bacon, Lenice Ingram. *American Patchwork Quilts*. New York, New York: William Morrow & Company, Inc., 1973.

Beyer, Jinny. *The Quilters Album of Blocks and Borders*. McLean, Virginia: EPM Publications, Inc., 1980.

Burnham, Dorothy K. *Pieced Quilts of Ontario*. Toronto, Ontario: ROM.

Capper's Weekly. Topeka, Kansas: April 1971.

The Encyclopedia of Collectibles, Buttons to Chess Sets. Alexandria, Virginia: Time-Life Books, 1978.

Finley, Ruth E. *Old Patchwork Quilts and the Women Who Made Them*. Philadelphia: J. B. Lippincott Company, 1929.

Godey's Lady's Book. New York: The Godey Company, 1852.

Graham, Elinor. *The Maine Charm String*. New York: MacMillan, 1946.

Hall, Carrie A. and Kretsinger, Rose G. *The Romance of the Patchwork Quilt in America*. New York: The Caxton Printers, Ltd., 1935.

Horton, Laurel and Myers, Lynn Robertson. *Social Fabric; South Carolina's Traditional Quilts*. South Carolina: McKissock Museum, 1985.

In Praise of Patchwork, Mt. Vernon, Illinois: Mitchell Museum, 1979.

Influences: Traditional and Contemporary Quilts. Wheatridge, Colorado: Leman Publications, Inc., 1983.

National Button Bulletin, National Button Society, Kentucky, September 1948.

Orlofsky, Patsy and Myron. *Quilts in America*. New York: McGraw-Hill Book Company, 1974.

Palenske, Bess Torian. *The Charm String*. New York: American Book Company, 1943.

Peacock, Primrose. *Antique Buttons*. New York: Drake Publishers, Inc., 1972.

Pullan, Mrs. *The Lady's Manual of Fancy-Work*. New York: Dick and Fitzgerald, 1859.

Quilter's Newsletter Magazine. Wheatridge, Colorado: Leman Publications, March 1980.

Roberts, Catherine. *Who's Got the Button?*. New York: David McKay Company, Inc., 1962.

Wallaces' Farmer, January 18, 1929.

Webster, Marie D. *Quilts, Their Story and How to Make Them*. New York: Doubleday, Page and Company, 1915.

ACKNOWLEDGMENTS

I wish to express my sincere thanks to those who helped me in the writing of this book. Dan Ramsey has once again done a superb job of illustrating, and the excellent photographs by Steve Tuttle add a special touch.

Numerous people have helped me with the research and I wish to thank Jane Adams, past Editor of the *National Button Bulletin*; Cuesta Benberry; Barbara Brackman; Mona Clark; Gail M. Getz, Associate Curator, Decorative Arts, The State Museum of Pennsylvania; Lesly-Claire Greenberg; Joyce Gross, Editor of *Quilters' Journal*; Sue Hannan; Linda Horton; Carter Houck, Editor of *Lady's Circle Patchwork Quilts*; Bonnie Leman, Editor, *Quilter's Newsletter Magazine*; Kay Lettau; Nancy Shea; Mildred Smith; Dorothy Harvey, Editor, *Capper's Weekly*; Yoko Sawanobori and Ellen Swanson.

Many other people allowed me to use photographs of their beautiful quilts in the book. I wish to thank Barbara Bockman, Fay Goldey, Kathryn Kuhn, Diana Leone, Lenore Parham, Linda Pool, Susan Powers, Jay Romano, Judy Spahn and Ellen Swanson.

Photographs not credited to a museum have been made by Steve Tuttle of Photo Works West, Alexandria, Virginia.

J.B.